PAT
HADEN

MY ROOKIE SEASON WITH THE LOS ANGELES RAMS

PAT HADEN

MY ROOKIE SEASON WITH THE LOS ANGELES RAMS

by PAT HADEN *with*
ROBERT BLAIR KAISER

WILLIAM MORROW AND COMPANY, INC.

NEW YORK   1977

Printed in the United States of America.

Library of Congress Cataloging in Publication Data

Haden, Pat.
    Pat Haden: my rookie season with the Los Angeles Rams.

    1. Haden, Pat. 2. Football players—United States—Biography. 3. Los Angeles. Football club (National League) I. Kaiser, Robert Blair, joint author.
GV939.H24A36   796.33'2'0924 [B]   77-9441
ISBN 0-688-03224-9

BOOK DESIGN   CARL WEISS

FOR

MY MOTHER AND FATHER,

JIM, PAUL, KATHLEEN, STACEY,

WHO HAVE ALWAYS KNOWN ABOUT ME—

AND FOR

CINDY, WHO IS LEARNING

PROLOGUE

LIVING IN SOUTHERN CALIFORNIA IN THE LATE SIXTIES, I couldn't help taking special note of a young man named Patrick Capper Haden. When I first heard of him, he was playing high school football with J. K. McKay, the son of Coach John McKay of the University of Southern California. Because of the USC connection, Haden and young McKay drew a good deal of press attention, and justified all the ink with decidedly winning ways. McKay caught the passes, Haden threw them, and their team, a Catholic school in the San Gabriel Valley, beat everyone in sight. In their senior year, they won the CIF Playoffs (that is, the championship of Southern California) in the L.A. Coliseum.

It was no surprise when Haden and McKay entered USC together. And no surprise to see them star there, beating Notre Dame in a couple of thrillers and playing in three consecutive Rose Bowl games. In the closing seconds of their last Rose Bowl game, against Ohio State, before 102,000 spectators (and 75 million more watching on TV), Haden

7

threw a long pass to McKay for the winning touchdown. SC was mainly a running ballclub, the alma mater of O. J. Simpson, Clarence Davis, Sam Cunningham, A. D. Davis. Even so, Haden had set a number of passing records at Troy; that's why the Los Angeles Rams drafted him in the winter of 1975. I had seen Haden as a winner. I guessed that the Rams did, too.

But there were others who also saw in Pat Haden something special. The American Rhodes Committee gave him a coveted Rhodes Scholarship, two years at one of the world's great universities, Oxford, to study anything he pleased. For that, Pat turned his back on the Rams and went off to England—after pocketing a $35,000 bonus to play a larking summer season with the Southern California Sun of the World Football League.

But then, in the summer of 1976, Pat Haden was back in California, under contract with the Rams. He had decided to take a half-year's leave from Oxford and give the National Football League a try. Many football fans wondered about that move. Some said Pat Haden was too small to make it in the NFL. Furthermore, he seemed outclassed by two other veteran quarterbacks on the Rams, James Harris and Ron Jaworski. Pat Haden seemed to be trading his golden opportunities at Oxford (and maybe an early start on a law career) for a seat way down on the end of the Rams' bench. The experts said it would be some years before he'd be a regular.

I didn't agree. I knew Haden was a winner. Somehow, I thought, Pat Haden will prove himself—and in his rookie season at that. And if he does, I thought, I would like to write a chronicle of how he does so. Not only am I a football nut, I am also interested in the psychology of success—in what separates the "winners" from the "losers."

In early August I dropped Haden a note. "I have a hunch," I wrote, "that you will have a very interesting season as a

Ram—and that, by season's end, a writer like me will wish that you'd had the foresight to record your struggle in a diary . . . in some kind of day-by-day account. . . . If you end up the season as the Rams' number one quarterback (as I'm betting you will), we could have . . . a very fine book."

More than a week passed before Haden replied to my note. He said we ought to talk. Could I come down to the Rams' training camp in Orange County, over twenty miles southeast of Los Angeles? I found that he was cautious about his first-year chances with the Rams and I agreed that maybe it was too much to hope that a rookie would end up the season as number one. "But that doesn't matter," I said. "Whether you play or not, I think people will be interested in your particular view of a season with the Rams."

Pat nodded and said he'd like to keep some notes on the season. He'd been keeping a diary at Oxford. When I saw that diary, I was more interested in him than ever. Pat was a good observer and wasn't afraid to express some of his own feelings about what went on around him.

Not far into the diary, I found Pat comparing the social contributions made by teachers or doctors or agricultural specialists to those of a quarterback in the National Football League. He felt guilty (under the challenges of his fellow Rhodes Scholars) about the kind of money he had made the previous summer playing for the Southern California Sun. He agonized over his decision to return to the U.S. as "a gridiron entertainer, no more." But then I found him temporizing, in a very human way, by deciding to meet the Rams' challenge.

"I am aspiring," he wrote, "to do something—play quarterback on a Super Bowl contender—that only a few men in the world can do. And I'll only be doing that for a short time. The average pro football career lasts three years. Mine won't last more than ten. By then, somewhere between three and

9

ten, I'll be a lawyer. And maybe a little later I will launch a career in politics as well—not because I have any kind of thirst for power, but because it would be a way for me to serve others."

But Pat wasn't even sure he wanted a career in the law or in politics. He was very much an unfinished man. When he applied for his Rhodes Scholarship, he'd told the screening committee what he was looking for at Oxford:

> I do not consider myself an intellectual. I get good grades, but I work hard. I honestly feel my academic growth has been very limited. I have been so concerned with getting good grades and so occupied with football that I have not done enough to enrich my intellect. I hope that a Rhodes Scholarship will allow me to do this. I would like to have the free time and a free mind to write poetry, to study contemporary literature and to look into other things I enjoy, like music—things that I would like to pursue but have not been able to at the University of Southern California. I have spent so much time as an undergraduate with busywork, playing games, and trying to get A's that I have not really been educated.

Through the pages of Pat's Oxford diary, I could see that he was following through with that resolve. Besides "reading" economics, politics and philosophy, he immersed himself in the culture and conversation of Oxford and London. He enjoyed Tschaikowsky's *Sleeping Beauty,* as performed by the London Festival Ballet, visited Westminster Abbey and the British Museum and the National Gallery, and played on the Oxford volleyball team with an international cast: two Canadians, two Germans, a Czech, a Singapore Chinese and three Englishmen.

He also broadened himself by traveling extensively on the Continent with four other American Rhodes Scholars: Andy Savitz, a Bostonian who had been student body president at Johns Hopkins; Mike McCaffery, who had been captain of

10

the swimming team at Princeton; Griff Harsh, a blueblood from Alabama who had graduated first in his class at Harvard; and Chris Peisch, who had been captain of the track team at Dartmouth.

In France, Pat marveled, with Andy Savitz, over the cathedral in Rouen: "To think of the dedication that went into the building of this marvelous cathedral and what it represented! Maybe if we had this kind of dedication, life wouldn't seem quite so irrelevant." And in Honfleur, a seaport town on the Brittany coast, he stood on the quay, watched the rhythm of activity and thought a good deal about the kind of occupations that make a life worthwhile: "The men fished all day long, scooping up plaice, halibut and flounder in their modest nets, and then chugged back into port in the afternoon. That was a signal for their wives to descend upon them, stack the catch in their baskets, then sell it in the streets while the fishermen checked their nets for tears and folded them up again for another expedition on the following day. Not an exciting life, certainly. But the people have good strong, happy faces. I would be surprised to learn that any of them are discontented with their lot."

On Omaha Beach, the scene of the Allied invasion of June 6, 1944, nine years before Pat was born, Pat looked over the rows upon rows of white crosses and Stars of David and wondered "how many thousands of shattered dreams were represented here, what unrealized potentials, how many broken hearts and grieving families."

Pat and his friends didn't spend all of their travel time looking over the required historical sites. They frequented sidewalk cafés, challenged some Frenchmen to a "fooseball" tournament in a bar at Avignon, gambled at the casino in Monte Carlo and got smashed at a little hotel in Innsbruck. But in Munich, on Christmas Eve, they attended midnight Mass and then, the next morning, visited Dachau, a former

11

Nazi extermination camp. There, they looked at the labs where Nazi scientists used human guinea pigs for experiments designed to test the limits of human endurance and wandered through displays of photographic blowups, pictures of men, women and children being marched off to be killed.

Seeing maybe a hundred of these blowups was the limit of my endurance. I was studying one grainy shot of a group of children no more than five or six years old and the thing I noticed most about them was their eyes: the camera had frozen their eyes in darting sidelong glances, each of the kids looking a different way, as if they *knew* something was happening but they weren't quite sure what it was or where it was coming from. But I put myself in the middle of this group and *I* knew and I almost threw up on the spot. Andy, my Jewish friend from Boston who almost took communion last night, was right at my side. He broke down and began weeping and then his tears turned into great uncontrollable sobs. Mike and I helped him into the van and we got the hell out of there. A sign at the gate said in several languages: NEVER AGAIN. Amen.

For three hours or more we did not speak to one another. I could not believe what man has done to his fellow man. And yet I know that even today, somewhere, men are capable of similar atrocities.

Pat's Oxford diary ended on an upbeat note; I later learned this was typical of Haden, who is always expecting the best from everyone—and usually getting it:

Oxford was a humbling, exciting, enlightening experience. The people everywhere were incredibly interesting. The world is a big place, much bigger than the one I knew on the cozy campus of Southern Cal. There is a lot to be done and, because I have been so overprivileged, a lot I can and want to do. I never realized how much is possible. I can change the world.

That diary did it for me. I told Pat that I definitely wanted to spend some time with him every week throughout the

12

season. "I don't know what we'll produce," I said. "But I think it will be more than worthwhile."

He was pleased. But he repeated what he had told me before, that I was taking quite a gamble on him because "rookie quarterbacks don't play too much on the really good teams in the league."

"Maybe so," I said. "But you never can tell."

"Yes," said Haden. "I am a very lucky guy. Good things happen to me. I make things happen."

As it turned out, Pat Haden did make things happen. He had more than an interesting season and he did end up by-passing two quarterbacks who could throw better, farther, faster than he. One of them was a national hero, the first black man to make it as a quarterback in the NFL. The other was a favorite of the reporters who covered the Rams, a good raconteur and one of the most popular members of the club. A rookie who was less level headed than Haden might have destroyed the team and created riots in a football-mad city where the selection of a Rams quarterback triggers much more interest than the selection of a mayor. Haden did not do that. The Great Quarterback Controversy still raged in Southern California, but the Rams accepted Haden, and under his field leadership they came within six inches of getting to the Super Bowl. Here is Haden's story of how it all happened.

ROBERT BLAIR KAISER
Mammoth Lakes, California

July 11

I DROVE A LONG TENSE DRIVE TO FULLERTON THIS AFTER-
noon in my leased blue Pinto, out the Pomona Freeway
toward Diamond Bar, through the parched Brea Canyon and
on down the Orange Freeway. I had a lot of time to worry
about how things would go for me. More than a year ago I
had a good experience at the Ram rookie and quarterback
camp, but I knew this camp would be different. At the rookie
camp, James Harris and Ron Jaworski were very kind to me
and very helpful. But I wasn't a threat to them then. They
knew I was going to Oxford. Now here I am again, and this
time I'm after their jobs. How will they treat me now?

I found the Rams headquarters just north of campus, the
University Village Apartments. They were on Oxford Street.
A good omen, maybe? I parked my car, grabbed my bag and
wandered up toward a cluster of white two-story buildings:
Jack Teele, the team's v.p. and traveling secretary, came right
up to me with a smile and handshake to welcome me to camp.
Near the cafeteria Jack and I stopped in front of a large
bulletin board, where the camp announcements and schedule
were posted. I found my name on the list, "Haden, Pat, #11,
Room 243." Number eleven is a QB's number. I assumed
that was mine. Yes, there was John Cappelletti's, Number 22,
and Lawrence McCutcheon's, Number 30. Naturally, I

couldn't have my SC number, 10, because the Rams place kicker, Tom Dempsey, already had it. I noted that sixty-one men were due in camp tonight, forty-two rookies and nineteen vets, with twenty-five more vets scheduled in later in the week.

Teele told me we were all divvied up five men to a suite and that everyone with me would be a rookie. "We've got more rookies than usual this year," Teele said. Yeah, I thought, forty-two of them. And how many would stick? A half dozen or so? Many of these guys were the cream of last year's seniors—and so few of them would last. I found three others in the suite. They didn't seem very friendly—possibly because they resented my apparently privileged status: I'd been assigned the only private bedroom in the suite.

The chow was good; plain, served cafeteria style but plentiful. Steak and baked potatoes, as much as we wanted, and salad. I had two steaks (better stoke up for tomorrow), but went easy on the potatoes. At Oxford the diet was all too starchy.

Coach Knox, dressed in slacks and a screaming sport shirt, said a few words of welcome after dinner, told us about the daily schedule and gave us a little pep talk about the Rams. Knox is proud of his record in L.A., thirty-four wins, eight losses in three years; and three straight division titles. "We're successful," he said, "because we're intelligent, we're well drilled, we stress fundamentals. And our coaching staff is the best in the league."

After dinner I looked at the schedule again. Gee, I thought, this is like being in the army. Now, I am not surprised to learn that Coach Knox idolizes three tough coaches: Vince Lombardi, Bear Bryant and Don Shula.

Wakeup	7:00
Breakfast	7:30

(attendance mandatory at all meals,
names checked at cafeteria door)

16

Dress up	8:30
On field	9:30
Off field	11:15
Lunch	12:00
Tape and dress	1:30
On field	2:30
Off field	4:15
Dinner	6:00
Meetings	7:00 to 10:00
Lights out	11:00

These were grown men, many of them married. And they couldn't even sleep with their wives? Somebody next to me said, "We get two nights off, Wednesdays and Saturdays."

"Yeah," I said, "I should think so. I mean for one who has normal sex drives—"

One of the others—a veteran, I guess—interrupted. "The Rams have more than normal sex drives," he said.

July 12

WHEN I GOT OVER TO THE LOCKER ROOM, THE TRAINER, Gary Tuthill, put me on a scale and I found I didn't weigh more than 173 pounds. The food at Oxford was worse for me than I thought. And so was the regime. I'd done some running (not nearly enough), played some volleyball and a little cricket, but I should have been lifting weights, which I hate to do.

"Most of the Rams are on a weight program," said Tuthill, "and I expect you'll want to go on one, too." It was a statement and a question. I assured Tuthill that I would. What would he suggest? He said he thought I should spend two

17

nights a week at a gym near the college, and he gave me six basic exercises to do on three different Nautilus weight machines. "These will help build up your triceps, your pectorals and upper shoulders," he said. "You'll see. Maybe help you gain a little weight, too."

A few of us started out to the field at 9 A.M., wearing shorts and jerseys, cleats and helmets, cracking jokes about the glory boys in the NFL, the quarterbacks, who not only got most of the headlines and the biggest salaries, but were given signal treatment even in camp: everyone else had white jerseys on, the QB's had red ones. Hands off the quarterbacks.

But then two police cars came roaring up with their sirens on. "There's some kind of nut loose on campus," said one of the cops. "Shot seven people already. You guys better get back in the locker room." Ah, Southern California, epitome of the American dream. Only trouble is, those who don't fulfill their dreams of riches and romance must live side by side with those whose fulfillments get more than ample coverage in the media. No wonder the unbalanced sometimes start shooting those around them.

A half hour later we got an "all clear" and, a little more soberly now, trooped out to the field. I thought that I was in fair shape. I'd been throwing passes to my friends at Oxford. But that wasn't nearly good enough. My friends there didn't have pro speed and I found that whenever I threw the ball here I was way behind my receivers.

Practices were incredibly well organized. No standing around for anybody, one drill after another, under the direction of nine coaches, lots of hard work. Lots of running. And then, at night, plenty of classroom study. The Rams' offense is not much different from the Sun's or SC's: one quarterback, two running backs, one tight end, two wide receivers. But it's all done from so many different formations

18

—and against so many different defenses—that it quickly becomes very complicated.

By ten P.M. I was ready for the rack. I talked with my roommates for a while, but could hardly keep my eyes open. My roomies are Carl Ekern, a six three, 220-pound linebacker from San Jose State (and a fifth-round draft choice), Joe Fabien, a wide receiver from Cal State Fullerton and two other QB's, both of them big strong guys: Steve Hamilton, six four, 196, from Emporia State, and Jerry Dyer, six five, 196, from Santa Ana College and Southern Utah. The three of us are fighting for one lousy job, third-string QB. We talk as if we each have an equal shot at it, but I think Jerry and Steve, both nice guys, are deluding themselves. They are not going to make it. What will they do when they get cut? I doubt they even want to think about it.

July 13

I AM AMAZED AT THE CLOSE ATTENTION THE RAMS COACHES give to every detail. They've got a cameraman who shoots the practices—every day. By the end of summer camp someone says they'll have more than ten miles of film. Today Mickey Ducich filmed closeups on each of the rookie quarterbacks' hands as we took the snap from center. Fifteen minutes for each of us, under the supervision of Kenny Myer, who handles the quarterbacks.

Then, a little farther away from us, he focused on the receivers, with their coach Leeman Bennett. Lee, a quarterback himself in college, has them catching his short passes, turn-ins, slants, hooks, sidelines, as the camera watches. Lee aims the ball at their ankles and they reach down and grab it off their shoetops. He aims it high over their heads and they go up for it. If somebody drops the ball, Lee shouts what is already obvious: "You dropped it. You dropped it." Anything a receiver can touch he can catch; dropping it is *his* responsibility.

Tonight, at the quarterback meeting, we watched the rushes: nothing but handoffs for forty-five minutes, with a running commentary by Myer. I would rather have been watching "Welcome Back, Kotter."

Chuck Knox never goes up on the one hundred-foot tower behind our south end zone to oversee the others. But he does seem to give more autonomy to his assistant coaches than John McKay did at USC and he is depending, it seems, on Kenny and Lee to put together most of the offense. Kenny was offensive coordinator for the New York Jets when Knox was an assistant there. Lee worked with Knox when Chuck moved on to the Detroit Lions. I know I can learn a lot from both of them.

July 14

JAMES HARRIS AND RON JAWORSKI WERE HERE AT CAMP FOR dinner tonight. Both of them, I can see, are immensely popular with the squad, and there doesn't seem to be any racial split on the Rams—nothing like the blacks gravitating to Harris and the whites to Jaworski.

We had a quarterback meeting tonight and afterward Harris took me aside for a little talk. At six four and 225, he is a little bigger than I had remembered him. He must have assumed that I wouldn't be here unless I wanted his job

20

—and that I wouldn't be worth a damn if I didn't. But he couldn't have been kinder to me. "Look," he said, "if you need any help from me, if there's anything you don't understand and you don't want to ask the coaches, you come to me. I'll help you any way I can."

James Harris is a helluva guy and I will take all the help he can give me. Then what happens if I get his job? I know: it takes two or three years for a good college quarterback to make it in the NFL. But I feel something good's going to happen to me—this year. I don't know *what*. Maybe somebody will get traded. But good things always happen to me. I've come to expect them.

In high school I was fortunate to attend Bishop Amat at a time when they had a group of super athletes; we went to the CIF Finals twice. In college, I was lucky to be at SC at just the right time, when they needed a quarterback, and to have great receivers like John McKay, Lynn Swann and Shelton Diggs. I could have played behind somebody else for most of my college career (like UCLA's Jeff Dankworth did when he played understudy to John Sciarra). And I was lucky enough to be at SC with some other super athletes, like A. D. Davis and Richard Wood, who helped take us to three straight Rose Bowls.

Even working summers, I was lucky. I got a job as a Hollywood extra, along with Johnny McKay, and, invariably, I'd get picked out of the crowd for a speaking part. There were sixty of us standing around one day on location for a movie called *The Blue Knight,* a police picture with William Holden and George Kennedy, when a director said, "Hey, you, the kid with the blond hair. We want you for a special sequence." He wanted *me*. Instead of making an extra's wages, $35 a day, I'd be making $100. Not bad.

But that's the way things have always worked for me. My family couldn't afford to send me to SC. My father was a salesman for a medical supply house, never very well paid. My mother did some secretarial work. But there I was. In four years I got an education worth some $25,000, a good education, made some fine friends who'll be my friends forever, played big-time football for a major power and got lots of exposure on national TV. It all added up to this good fortune. I got preferential treatment wherever I went. I felt a little guilty. What did I really do to deserve it all?

I give thanks for my family. My dad always gave me lots of moral support. So did my mother. She'd been a star tennis player herself before she had her five children and she wanted us to excel, too. When I was growing up in Scottsdale, Arizona, and West Covina, California, Mom would drive me and my Little League teammates to three, four, five baseball games a week. And, when I was playing Pop Warner football, my two older brothers, Jim and Paul, would play with me by the hour, catch my passes until they were ready to drop, make me stretch my abilities to the ultimate. And, maybe more important than anything, they helped me believe in myself. "You can do it, Pat." They repeated it so often I ended up knowing that I could do it. Do what? Anything I wanted.

For a short time, I think my brothers and sisters resented my success. When I got my scholarship to SC, my dad, figuring my college education would cost him nothing, bought me a car. The other kids were a little jealous of that. But that feeling wore off. Now my family gives me nothing but encouragement and, with that, I need very little more to keep me going.

July 14

WE HAD OUR FIRST SCRIMMAGE TODAY, CAMERAS WHIRRING away. One of the cameras sits high atop the tower behind the south goal post. I went the whole way at quarterback and completed almost every pass I threw. But I know that, tough as the scrimmages are, games are tougher. I overheard Jack Youngblood telling one writer, "A game is about six times as intense as this."

In Youngblood's case I can believe that. He was voted the NFC's top defensive player last season and the Most Valuable Player on the Rams. I have never seen a pass rush like his and Fred Dryer's. At six four and 240, Jack is probably no bigger or smaller than any of the other defensive ends in the league, but on him the sinew and muscle seem distributed more like a swimmer's. I'd guess Jack has a fifty-six-inch chest and a thirty-inch waist, no hips at all, and, with the finely chiseled features of a statue by Phidias, almost too handsome to be, ahem, a lineman.

The main thing about Jack is that he's fast; he runs around pass blockers rather than through them. And he still gets to the quarterback before the poor son of a gun has time to get rid of the ball. He had fourteen sacks last year.

Jack is really Herbert Jackson Youngblood, III, no relation to Jim Youngblood, one of our linebackers, and he grew up packing watermelons and punching cattle on the family ranch in Monticello, Florida. Jack was an All-American at the University of Florida and a number one draft choice of the Rams in 1971. Judging from what I have heard from him so far, I'd say he is very intelligent. No wonder that he's been elected to the executive board of the NFL Players' Association.

Fred Dryer, our defensive end on the other side, is built like Youngblood, tall (six six), broad-shouldered, slim-hipped: both of them epitomize the new, faster, streamlined lineman of the 1970's. Dryer also got fourteen sacks last year and in the big playoff win against St. Louis, it was Dryer who threw the key block enabling Jack Youngblood to go all the way, forty-seven yards, with a TD pass interception. Both Youngblood and Dryer made the Pro Bowl squad last year.

Fred has many facets. He was raised in Southern California, likes to surf and ski and come and go as he pleases. In 1972, the year he moved to the Rams (after three years with the New York Giants), Fred lived in a Volkswagen van, drank wheat germ and celery cocktails and was tagged by the press as something of a nut. He did little to counter that impression when he and Lance Rentzel "covered" the Super Bowl for *Sport* magazine in 1975. They wore comic suits and snap-brim hats with PRESS stuck in their hatbands and asked silly, tongue-in-cheek questions at all the press conferences. In other words, they were having fun. As a result, however, a New York writer wrote the NFL commissioner, demanding the pair be reprimanded. Rozelle had too much of a sense of humor to do that and the matter died.

I guess Freddie is one of the most well-rounded guys on the squad. His years in New York have made him more worldly wise than some on the team. He reads a lot and has spent five off-seasons writing a book about his life in pro football; in fact, he's still working on it. "I'm fortunate to be able to play here," he told me. "I'll probably be a ten- or twelve-year man. But this is only one block of time in my life, phase one. I have a lot of other plans." Dryer is building a spa, a big one,

4,700 square feet, down in Mission Viejo. And he has a small apartment house down there, too.

I am finding that many of the Rams have business minds and are getting a jump on their futures even while they seem to be men playing a boys' game. Larry Brooks, who plays next to Dryer in the front four, is an executive trainee at the Union Bank. Merlin Olsen is an entrepreneur with varied business interests, most notably a Porsche-Audi agency in the Valley.

One of the reasons why the Rams get ahead: we have an owner, Carroll Rosenbloom, who takes pleasure in helping them do so. C.R. (as he is known to his friends) set up many Baltimore Colts in business when he owned the Colts and, without a lot of fanfare, he does the same thing for many of the Rams. The Rams, in turn, I am told, have a lot of loyalty to C.R. and to the team. Those who couldn't give it, or wouldn't give it, are long gone. And maybe that's one reason why the Rams are such a great group. The selfish guys just didn't fit in.

July 15

I WAS STRUCK BY THE REALIZATION THAT WE SPEND MORE time in the classroom than we do on the field. In our T-shirts and shorts, we come in and wedge ourselves into these little chairs and slap our looseleaf playbooks on the writing arms on the right and we listen—more intently I would guess than we ever did in college. But this is not higher education. It is war, and our coaches are like generals in the U.S. Army:

they talk strategy and tactics constantly and they keep giving us a tremendous amount to absorb.

The quarterbacks are the guys who have to soak up the most, because though the plays will be called from the side-lines, the quarterbacks will be expected to change those calls every so often. If the QB comes out of the huddle and finds the particular defensive alignment either threatens the probable success of the coaches' call or opens up a better possibility, then he has to change the call to an audible at the line of scrimmage. Coach Knox said today, "We're going to have a lot of audibles this year. Whether or not we use them will depend on the quarterbacks. If they're sharp enough and ballsy enough, they'll have lots of opportunities to do so—not to get us out of a bad play but to give us a better one."

This year, Knox says, the Rams' coaches will send in all the plays by a complicated set of wig-wag signals from the sidelines. In the past Knox sent in all the plays by shuttling a running back, either Jim Bertelsen or John Cappelletti. Now the plan is for Leeman Bennett to sit high atop the stadium in a booth near the press box.

Bennett will have an obvious advantage over the coach on the field. In his special box he will have the written game plan stretched out in front of him on a desk where, in any crisis, he can quickly find the precise plays the coaches decided during the week would work in given situations against this particular team. He will also have immediate access to Polaroid pictures of every play, which will be shot from the box by our photographer, John Trump, who is also a Ram scout. The Polaroids will give him the opportunity to take "another look" at the way opposing defenses are setting up against our various formations.

Helped by this information (and by his own fourteen years of coaching experience) Bennett will be in a theoretically better position to call the plays than any of the quarterbacks

26

or the coaches on the field. As the season progresses we shall see.

Once Bennett selects the play, he phones it down to Kenny Myer. Then Myer will semaphore the play to the QB. The signals look a lot like those of a third-base coach in baseball: right arm out, left arm out, a pat on the hat, a salute, skin to skin (hand to hand, maybe, or hand to cheek), skin to cloth (index finger to pants leg), a wave, legs spread, arms up, arms down.

Can other teams steal our signals? I doubt it. Some of the signals are "live" and others are "fake." How can the other team tell? A signal may be live if Myer is pointing at Knox and fake if he touches his knee first. Or fake if he's moving his feet and live if he's not. The feeling is that it's too much trouble—and too distracting—for the other team to steal our signals. We'll see about that, too. If we suspect that any team is doing it, there are ways to burn them—badly.

July 16

I HAD A LITTLE TALK WITH STEVE PREECE AFTER DINNER. Steve is one of our best athletes, a former all Pac-8 QB for Oregon State under Dee Andros, and a guy who does everything for us. He's a defensive safety, holder on extra points and field goals, member of the kickoff team and emergency backup QB. But he's been shaded by Dave Elmendorf and Bill Simpson at safety and he tells me he's playing out his option this year. That means he will be a free agent, and can sign on next season with any club in the NFL that wants him.

Why leave the Rams? I asked. He said it wouldn't be easy. "I've played for New Orleans, Philadelphia and Denver," he

27

said, "and I've talked to a lot of other players in the league. The Rams have the best organization anywhere. Few other teams see much of their owners. Carroll Rosenbloom takes a personal interest in each of us, talks to us all the time, makes sure we're happy. He even flies with us on the team plane. I don't know of any other owner who does that."

So why does Steve want to leave the Rams? He feels he can play first-string safety for at least a dozen teams in the NFL—and wants to do that before he gets too old. I can understand that. He is twenty-nine. If I am not first string by the time I am twenty-five or twenty-six, I'll be gone from the game forever, I think.

But I don't really know. Pro football is a funny game and nobody ever knows from one season to the next if he'll be playing—or where. The papers say that O. J. Simpson has given the Buffalo Bills an ultimatum: trade him to a club on the West Coast or he'll quit. He'd prefer playing in his old stomping grounds for the Rams and if that happens then some of the Rams will be moving to Buffalo—whether they'd planned on it or not. There's an uneasiness about this in camp. The players are kidding McCutcheon about it, telling him he'll like the snow and ice in Buffalo, and they're kidding Jack Youngblood and Jack Reynolds and Mike Fanning, too, because they are also guys Buffalo Owner Ralph Wilson reportedly wants and needs if he is going to give up O.J. Mainly defensemen. They're the guys who win most of the ball games in the NFL.

It takes a lot of chutzpah for O.J. to make a demand like this. He may be the only guy in the league who can do it. Others may have nearly as much talent. But none has O.J.'s flair—or his sense of self-enjoyment. If Harris had that, I wouldn't have a chance to beat him.

July 16

FULLERTON IS A GOOD WAYS AWAY FROM THE OCEAN, ORANGE
County, desert country, so the days get hot, up in the nine-
ties. And this schedule is a bitch. Same thing almost every
day. And, no matter how you do today, it's going to be the
same thing tomorrow. I am looking forward to Saturday
night, when I go home to Cindy. We have only been married
twenty days and I've been away seven of them already. I miss
her.

Some of the drudgery is necessary, I guess, but the coaches
have a favorite drill, called "seven on seven," that I like. Center, quarterback, two running backs, tight end and two wide
receivers go against three linebackers, two corner men and
two safeties. No tackling, lots of throwing. Lots of concentration needed here. The trick is to throw to the proper receiver at the proper time, no matter what the coverage, no
fumbles, no mistakes, over and over and over again. We call
29 FX post a hundred fifty times in July so that on some given
day in October or November the pattern will be as familiar
to us as our own faces in the mirror: Ron Jessie running a
short post, Harold Jackson running a deep post, Bob Klein
checking and driving toward the sideline and John Cappelletti
or Jim Bertelsen swinging the other way.

There is a duel going between John and Bert, and I think
John is winning right now, but it is hard to choose between
them. Both of them are better than average catchers and both
good blockers, too. In 1973 John was a Heisman Trophy
winner at Penn State. During '74 and '75, however, he spent
most of his time on the Rams bench. The sportswriters said

he was inexperienced. But *I* don't know how they expected him to get experience sitting on the bench. It looks like we are awfully deep this year in running backs. Besides McCutcheon, Bert, and John, we have Cullen Bryant, Rod Phillips, Rob Scribner, Jim Jodat and Mack Herron. We can only keep five, maybe six of them.

July 17

JAMES HARRIS IS A GREAT GUY. I DO NOT KNOW WHY THEY call him Shack. He says it is "a long story" and I can believe that. Shack is full of long stories, many of them excruciatingly funny ones, about his growing up in Monroe, Louisiana. Once (he takes about an hour to tell this), he held the great Elvin Hayes to fourteen points in a local basketball game. "Oh, yeah," he said last night, "I am still a legend in Monroe." He pronounced it MON-roe. "Whenever they play softball or basketball, they still choose me just in case I happen to show up in town that weekend."

But Monroe, Louisiana, was and still is Deep South, and I imagine that much of Shack's warm humor about the place is a cover for the bitterness he felt growing up in Jim Crow country. Schools were still segregated when he started down there, but breaking the color line at his high school couldn't have been that much fun, otherwise why did he end up going to Grambling, an all-black school?

Shack told me at practice that the coaches keep statistics on the quarterbacks in camp. "You mean," I said, "they tote up my completions, percentages and everything all through practice?"

Affirmative. According to Shack, Knox and his staff grade

every player in camp every day, spend a lot of the club's money on computer time and retain a statistician to provide them with analysis throughout the season. I almost got the impression that, to Knox, pro football is General Motors with shoulder pads and a band on Sunday. "So," said Shack, "if you want to look good on the stats, throw high percentage passes to your backs."

I appreciate this tip from Shack. But it also amazes me. What kind of a regime do we have here, where looking good is considered as important as *being* good?

July 19

THE RAMS HAVE A TERRIFIC ORGANIZATION, FROM TOP TO bottom, and it is obvious to me, after talking to many of the vets, that the Rams look for more than raw football ability. These guys are all intelligent, well spoken, and they have a lot of things going for them off the field. At dinner tonight, Tom Dempsey, our place kicker and a squad leader, insisted that I get up and sing the Oxford fight song. There is no Oxford fight song, so I sang the Trojan fight song, accompanied by a chorus of boos. This is how veterans are *supposed* to treat rookies in camp. Rookies are here to take jobs away from veterans.

After dinner, however, I had a good talk with Tom Mack, our veteran guard from Michigan, who has made the Pro Bowl nine of the ten years he's been in the NFL. Tom has a graduate degree in nuclear engineering and works six months a year with the Bechtel Corporation, one of the biggest construction companies in the world. He also organizes a golf tournament every summer for charity, with an assist from

Carroll Rosenbloom, who puts up the front money. In the last two years Tom has raised more than $30,000 for the Boy Scouts. I like Tom. Aside from the fact that I'm predisposed to liking anyone who is going to give protection to our quarterbacks, I find he's interested in a whole lot more than football. In June he helped campaign against the nuclear initiative, a measure that would have held up the building of a good many generating plants. "It was a bad idea," says Tom. "We need nuclear power."

July 20

I HEARD MERLIN OLSEN TELLING MIKE FANNING TODAY that "A good defensive lineman has to be part charging buffalo and part ballet dancer. And he has to know when to be each." Olsen is six five and 270. Fanning is six six and 260. Some ballet dancers. Ole has been teaching Mike, an All-American from Notre Dame, everything he's learned in fourteen years of pro ball. Mike will be taking over Ole's defensive tackle position next year, alongside Larry Books, now entering his fifth year with the Rams.

July 23

SOME OF US WATCHED THE COLLEGE ALL-STAR GAME tonight from Chicago because we have three Ram rookies on the squad, Jackie Slater, an offensive tackle from Jackson State, Kevin McLain, a linebacker from Colorado State, and

Ron McCartney, a linebacker from Tennessee. The Pittsburgh Steelers were killing the All-Stars, as expected, 24–0, when a cloudburst stopped the game in the third quarter. First time I've ever seen a football game called on account of rain.

July 24

WE HAD A GREAT SCRIMMAGE TODAY. THE ROOKIES HAD plenty of chances to show their stuff. Right now it looks like the Rams have more good rookies and second-year players than they bargained for, more than a full offensive team: Center Geoff Reece of Washington State, three guards, Dennis Harrah of Miami, Greg Horton of Colorado and Dan Nugent of Auburn. Two tackles, Doug France of Ohio State and Al Oliver of UCLA. Three wide receivers, Jerald Taylor of Texas A&I, Freeman Johns of SMU, and Dwight Scales of Grambling. A full backfield: me, Rod Phillips of Jackson State and Jim Jodat of Carthage. And then there are the three rookies who played in the All-Star game. McLain, McCartney and Slater checked in here this afternoon. They're going to have to hustle to catch up to the others.

I went most of the way at QB and felt I did well. Coach Myer said I showed poise, passing accuracy and good control in the huddle. But this only means that I'm the leading *rookie* QB in camp. Harris and Jaworski are still way ahead of me. Ron Jaworski is a pleasure to work with. He is always smiling, always charged up, always eager and ready to help me—and anyone else he can.

He has so much confidence that the *Herald-Examiner* recently did a feature on him called "JAWORSKI: AN ALI IN CLEATS." It quoted him as saying, "If I'm given a legitimate chance to win this job, I'll win it." Ron comes right out and says this to reporters. I can't talk this way to the press. I'm just a rookie. But privately I think I can win the job.

July 27

THE RAMS CUT SEVEN PLAYERS TODAY, INCLUDING TWO OF my roommates, Jerry Dyer, QB, and Joe Fabien, wide receiver. I didn't even get a chance to say good-bye. When I got back to my room after practice, they'd packed and departed.

This was picture day in Fullerton, a welcome break in our boring routine. We suited up in our blue and gold uniforms and did little numbers for the media—and for something called NFL Properties, run by the league. The NFL people put out game programs all season and posters, too, of each team's stars. The Rams who seem to rate posters this year: Merlin Olsen, Jack Youngblood, Fred Dryer, Isiah Robertson, Lawrence McCutcheon and James Harris.

July 28

KICKERS ARE A DING-Y LOT. TOM DEMPSEY, OUR PLACE-kicker and the record holder for his 63-yard kick against Detroit when he was playing for New Orleans in 1970, drinks beer like a prospector just come in from three weeks on the desert. Rusty Jackson, our punter, says he has aspirations of becoming a male nurse. And George Jakowenko, who is trying to win Dempsey's job, is a touchy guy who complains about the hold every time he misses a point-after-TD or a field goal. It's never his fault. Always mine. The reason kickers are ding-y is that they play under tremendous pressure. All too often a game is on the line with a single kick and rarely does the kicker get a second chance.

August 1

LAST NIGHT WE PLAYED OUR FIRST PRE-SEASON GAME AND drew 54,000 eager early birds to the Los Angeles Coliseum. Many of them, I am sure, wanted a first look at Coach John McKay's Tampa Buccaneers. Few expect the Bucs to win this year and almost everyone predicts a big season for the Rams, but Tampa gave us a good game and we only won 26–3.

Coach Knox had James Harris work the first half with Lawrence McCutcheon, Jim Bertelsen and John Cappelletti. All four of them looked great. Harris completed eleven of thirteen passes for 128 yards. McCutcheon averaged more than 7 yards on nine carries. Bert ran a dandy swing pass for 34 yards. John, playing only the second quarter, caught three for 37 yards and ran for 30 yards besides.

Neither Ron Jaworski, who played the third quarter, nor I, who played the fourth, brought the crowd to its feet. I ended with a respectable five for seven completions; I hit all my short, high percentage passes, missed on two long bombs and "guided" our third- and fourth-string backfield on a 45-yard TD drive.

John McKay, my old teammate at SC, did as well as any of the Bucs. He caught three from Steve Spurrier for 59 yards, not bad against our good secondary. After the game

John and I, walking down the familiar Coliseum tunnel, agreed that playing a no-sweat game like this was a far cry from our last mighty effort for Troy when we beat Ohio State in the Rose Bowl. "I goofed a couple of times," I told representatives of the local press in the dressing room. "But what the heck, it was my first time under the gun. It'll be a long season." I said I wanted to work a little harder on getting more zip on the ball, adding, "I'm not satisfied I have enough velocity."

August 8

COACH KNOX IS BRINGING ME ALONG SLOWLY. LAST NIGHT, against the fearsome defense of the Dallas Cowboys (who cleaned our clocks in the NFC championship game last year, 37–7), I didn't see any action at all. But Ron Jaworski did and he was super, leading the Rams to 234 yards and seventeen points in the first half as we beat the Cowboys 26–14.

Ron's 68-yard pass to Ron Jessie in the first quarter was a beauty: it went 55 yards in the air. And on our second TD drive, Ron rifled one to Jessie on a third and ten situation, then, on the next third down play, withstood a Dallas blitz and hit Harold Jackson for another crucial first down.

And John Cappelletti made the most of his first real shot at a starting job. Twelve carries for 75 yards, including one marvelous run up the left sideline in the first quarter, and three pass receptions. At six one and 217, John could be one of the best fullbacks in the league, because he can not only run and catch passes, he can block, too.

After the game Knox said, "We're not as good as we looked tonight." He's probably right. Dallas always goes a little easy in the preseason; there's nothing on it at all. Still, I think our defense intimidated Roger Staubach, who always plays to win. We held Roger to 100 yards passing and 3 yards running. But the coaches weren't about to tell the press how we did so and when the newspaper writers complained about that, Coach Knox said, "We might have to play these people again."

Kenny Myer, impressed with Ron's performance, told the press, "We have *two* good quarterbacks—and a third who ain't bad." I'll buy that.

August 13

SEATTLE. MY FIRST ROAD TRIP WITH THE RAMS, VIA A United Airlines charter. We worked out early this morning in Fullerton, then drove our own cars to United's freight terminal in L.A. for a 3 P.M. departure. We will spend tonight in Seattle and return to L.A. Saturday night after the game —which I am scheduled to start.

All the coaches and some members of the press sat in first class, all the players in back. In a lounge toward the rear of the plane, Harris, Jessie, Jackson, McCutcheon and Dr. Robert Kerlan, the team doctor, began a game of poker, and the cowboys, Jim Bertelsen, Ron Jaworski, Tom Dempsey, Jack Youngblood and Larry Brooks turned their tape deck up high on some country and western music. Toward the front, where I found a seat, Butch Robertson appropriated three seats across, covered them with a blanket and pillows and was preparing to take a nap. Butch, they say, is an active dude at night; he needs all the sleep he can get whenever he can find it. So off came his Cardin polo shirt and drawstring pants. No shorts. Butch stood there nude, hardly concerned about the stewardesses up front, pulling on a pair of tennis shorts and trading insults with Jack Reynolds. Before the plane had taxied down to the end of the runway he was asleep. No one else paid him any attention. The others, I guess, are used to Butch. And if you play weak side linebacker like Butch plays it, you can sleep anywhere and say anything you want.

They served a light lunch on the plane, but for supper we split for Seattle's better restaurants. Bob Klein and Rob Scribner and I and a few others went out to dinner and enjoyed insulting one another most of the evening. Klein is our big, veteran tight end, the only other player on the squad from SC; Scribner is a big gun in the Fellowship of Christian Athletes and a guy who seems to enjoy trading insults with me and Klein (because, I guess, we went to SC).

At UCLA, Scrib played quarterback as a freshman, linebacker as a sophomore, defensive back as a junior and in his senior year, wishbone quarterback. He is a hell of an athlete who can do anything, but he has had the same trouble finding a niche on the Rams as he did at UCLA. Last year, subbing for Jim Bertelsen, he carried forty-two times for 216 yards, a 5.1 average per carry, which isn't bad. Now he seems to spend most of his time on the special teams. He's also our fourth-string quarterback. In case Shack, Ron and I all get hurt.

The papers here are full of the Rams and the Seahawks. The new stadium, the Kingdome, where we worked out today, is a beauty and the Seahawks have already sold about fifty-eight thousand season tickets, some to fans as far away as Alaska, who will have to fly two and a half hours to see each game. The Seahawks must be the most successful first-year expansion franchise in any sport in any year in the history of success.

38

August 14

I WASN'T A BIT HAPPY WITH MY PERFORMANCE IN THE Kingdome, a narrow 16–13 victory for the Rams before a screaming crowd of 62,532. Nor were too many others on the club overjoyed. Oh, I threw five out of nine completions, but all my leadership amounted to was three fields goals in the first half (all the time allotted to me tonight). My longest pass, a 41-yarder to Dwight Scales, was underthrown and completed only because Dwight made a nice comeback on the ball.

On the whole our offense sputtered and stumbled. Why? Possibly because we were trying to do too much, using too many new plays, too many new players. In crucial situations, we'd lose 7 or 8 yards on a simple end run, the drive would falter and we'd have to settle for a field goal. I guess games like this are inevitable in the preseason. The coaches call sets of plays that will help them see how certain rookies do in a given game situation—whether those plays are appropriate or not. I know this is the right way to go about it because this allows our coaches to evaluate the talent under game conditions. Tonight, I am sure two guys won berths on the club: Freeman Johns and Dwight Scales; they each made three nice catches. Carl Ekern, the only roommate I have left, made four tackles and knocked down a pass. I think Carl's going to make it, too.

August 15

My last week's remark in the dressing room that I didn't have enough zip on the ball came back to haunt me this morning. In Bob Oates' game story for the L.A. *Times,* "Haden was throwing the ball accurately but without sufficient velocity." But except for the 41-yard completion I underthrew to Scales, I had enough velocity: the ball got there and the receiver caught it. What more could anyone want? Oates wrote that Harris' passes were better because they were faster. That ain't necessarily so.

Not everyone was so critical of my performance as Oates, however. Doug Krikorian of the *Herald-Examiner* gave all three QB's good marks and sympathized in print with the coach: "Poor Chuck! What's he going to do about this pressing problem? Too many quarterbacks. He has only four weeks left to resolve it." But Krikorian is being far too kind to me. So far I have given Coach Knox little reason to think of me as anything other than the QB who will run the upcoming opponent's offense each week in practice.

August 18

Don Klosterman, our general manager, was on the field watching us scrimmage this afternoon. He is amazing. A week ago, he was in the hospital recuperating from surgery so major he wasn't expected to live. Now here he is, laughing and joking with some reporters.

Klosterman was one of the best quarterbacks ever produced on the West Coast, had a brilliant career at Loyola University, starred in the East-West Shrine Game in San Francisco along with Frank Gifford and Hugh McElhenny and was just getting oriented to pro ball when he had a ski accident that was almost fatal. He was schussbooming down a trail when all of a sudden a girl darted in front of him. Rather than hit her, he veered off and went out of control into a clump of trees. They said he'd never walk again, but by sheer force of will he trained himself to do so, stayed in football as a general manager and ended up with Carroll Rosenbloom and the Rams. When the Rams drafted me, it was Klosterman who called to give me the news; he found me skiing at Aspen— and warned me to remember what happened to him.

August 22

BEFORE A SELLOUT CROWD OF 52,615 AT THE OAKLAND-Alameda County Coliseum, we beat the Raiders every which way last night, 23–14. They were three-point favorites and we spotted them seven points to begin with by letting Carl Garrett run back Tom Dempsey's opening kickoff 96 yards for a touchdown. But after that, with Harris running the team the first half and Jaworski the second (against Ken Stabler and Mike Rae, respectively), we beat the Raiders physically, mentally and emotionally.

We did it with an imaginative, wide-open offense that surprised Coach Knox's severest critics, the ones who have always claimed Knox was too conservative. He wasn't too conservative this night; he let Lee Bennett call a game that featured first-down passes, double reverses, screen passes, delayed

41

passes to wide receivers, fake double reverses, halfback option passes and even a shovel pass. It was, I think (or should have been), the culmination of a great preseason. We've been spending a lot of time in summer camp installing all these plays. As far as I'm concerned, we're finished. Bring on regular league play. Trouble is, we've got two more meaningless preseason games.

How is it that we could run and pass so well against a team many say will go to the Super Bowl? We did it up front. Our line beat their line, both ways, not only on defense (which isn't too surprising because we have the best defensive front in football) but on offense, too (which is surprising, because the Rams are minus two veteran linemen this year, Joe Scibelli and Charlie Cowan). But the rookies and second-year men have gladdened the heart of Coach Ray Prochaska.

Ray is fifty-six and has been coaching football for twenty-nine seasons, principally with the Nebraska Cornhuskers, the Chicago and St. Louis Cardinals, the L.A. Rams, under George Allen, the Cleveland Browns and now, again, with the Rams. He has one of the most exacting jobs on the club —and the least noticed. Unless and until the refs start calling us for holding; then everybody will wonder what the hell Prochaska is doing to earn his salary.

No one wondered last night. At one point in the second quarter, our best quarter against the Raiders, we had four rookies and a second-year man on our offensive line: Doug France, Greg Horton, Geoff Reece, Dan Nugent and Jackie Slater, and they all were sharp.

Another rookie came through, too. Our punter, Rusty Jackson, averaged 38.8 yards on six punts, hanging them up so high that Oakland returned them for a total of 13 yards. When Dalton Sherman Jackson was seven, back home in Centreville, Alabama, his dog died and he took it hard. He cried so fiercely and so long that his face seemed to take on a ruddy permanence. They finally called him "Rusty." At Louisiana State, he studied forestry, and last year he turned in such a good performance in the WFL that the Rams have given him a chance. He is the Rams' seventeenth kicker in ten years.

After the game, according to one newspaper report, Coach John Madden said, "To beat the Rams, you have to stop their running game and you have to be able to run yourself. We did neither and we lost."

Right on. Our defense held Mark Van Eeghen and Clarence Davis to a total of 30 yards—and the rest of the Raider runners to 55. Stabler and Rae together only got 150 in the air.

The plane trip back last night was fun. There seemed to be an extra supply of Coors aboard, the country and western music was up a decibel or two and Butch Robertson didn't even bother taking a nap—maybe this was because we only had a short flight home and because Butch was thinking about those *two* blondes waiting there at the airport for him in the big black limousine. As I say, this summer camp is just too long.

August 24

LAST YEAR RON JAWORSKI GOT A SALARY OF $29,700. HE told me today he could get a hell of a lot more if he signs a five-year contract with the Rams: $100,000 for 1976, and $20,000 more each and every season through 1980. A total of $700,000. He's turning it down, playing out his option and taking the $29,700. Unless, that is, he becomes our number one quarterback, in which case he'll sign another kind of contract. The guy's got confidence, I'll have to say that. If he doesn't make number one, he'll lose $70,300 this year.

August 26

THERE SEEMS TO BE LESS AND LESS OF AN ACTIVE SEASON
ahead for me. I'm absolutely bored by the monotony of this
summer camp—which is about two to four weeks too long
to suit me. I wonder if I'm putting out 100 percent. Or even
50 percent. One trouble is that I have a lot of things in my
future other than football. A boring drill, repeated for the
seventy-seventh time, is boring to the seventy-eighth power.

I think the coaches sense my feelings. They seem to have
no plans for me to play this Saturday night against Buffalo.
Not that they've *told me* that much. For bulletins, I read
Oates in the L.A. *Times*. He wrote a couple of days ago after
an interview with Coach Knox that I would play "little if any
more this season."

I wonder about that. There's still more talk about a big
trade with Buffalo for O. J. Simpson, talk that's heated up
again now that Ralph Wilson and the Bills have come to town.
The scuttlebutt is that Wilson will settle for McCutcheon,
Youngblood and Reynolds in return for O.J., but neither Knox
nor Rosenbloom will give up two of our blue-chip defensemen. Since that's so, maybe Jaworski would be part of another package. It is possible. Ron hasn't signed a contract—
and won't, until he sees whether he is going to do more than
sit on the bench all year. Maybe he'd be glad to go to Buffalo,
where he grew up.

My guess is that Ralph Wilson will, in the end, have to
take what we offer him. Otherwise, he may end up with no
O.J. and no other players either. I do not think O.J. is
bluffing.

August 29

WE BEAT BUFFALO LAST NIGHT IN THE COLISEUM 31–17—
proving that L.A. can play better football without O.J. than
Buffalo can. But disaster struck James Harris: he threw a
60-yard touchdown strike to Harold Jackson, but cracked his
thumb on the helmet of an onrushing lineman as he did so.
In the morning L.A. *Times* our team doctor, Robert Kerlan,
says Shack will be out for at least three weeks. In reading that
I got the chills: I had a premonition that something would
happen to change my status. But I sure as hell didn't want
anybody to get hurt.

For three games at least, Jaworski is the new number one
quarterback. And I'm number two. Now I'm glad we've got
some more exhibition games before we start the season September 12 in Atlanta. Ron (and I?) could use the game experience. I hope I get some this coming week against San
Francisco in the Coliseum. Under Monte Clark, the new
49ers look stronger than ever, particularly on defense.

September 5

I WAS SUPPOSED TO PLAY THE LAST QUARTER AGAINST SAN
Francisco last night. I got in for six plays. The final two, I had
instructions to fall on the ball—simply to preserve our 10–6

lead. There was a fearsome rush by their front four, Cleveland Elam, Jimmy Webb, Cedrick Hardman and Tommy Hart. They sacked Jaworski seven times.

But they didn't sack me. On one play where they might have, I scrambled for a 7-yard gain. I have 4.8 speed (in the 40-yard dash). I'm capable of running. I don't want to make a career out of it. But I can run when I need to.

We got a mere 166 yards rushing and 42 yards passing all night. We lost the ball three times on fumbles and once on an interception. And ran up 80 yards in penalties. We won because our defense was better (or luckier) than theirs. We intercepted Plunket four times. Monte Jackson * blocked a punt and ran 50 yards with it for our only TD.

The 49ers are damn good. "We didn't play under wraps," Knox told the press. "We used everything in our arsenal, a halfback pass, statue of liberty, shovel pass." Maybe now we won't congratulate ourselves too much about our great unbeaten (but largely meaningless) preseason. After this squeaker against the 49ers, we know we've got to buckle down for our opener against the Falcons in Jimmy Carter country.

---

* Editor's note: there are three Jacksons on the Rams: Rusty, a punter, Harold, a wide receiver, and Monte, a defensive safety. They are not related.

September 6

BLAIR FIELD, OWNED BY THE CITY OF LONG BEACH, IS A baseball stadium and that's what they use it for all summer. Come September, however, the Rams lease it. It's where I will be "going to work" every day from now until December, Monday through Saturday, from 8:30 A.M. to 4:30 P.M. That means I have to get up about 7 so I can make an 8:30 breakfast with Ron Jaworski and Shack Harris, then attend team meetings all morning until 12:30 P.M. Practice on Blair Field goes from 1 to 3 P.M. (because those are the hours when we generally play our games on Sunday). No lunch period. So Ron and Shack and I all have a good breakfast. We eat in the coffee shop of the municipal golf course right near Blair Field. The Ram offices are right upstairs: coaches' and scouts' rooms, film labs, the works, but they are nothing fancy. The coaches work here, they're not out to impress anyone.

Over at Blair Field, however, the Rams have an AAA-1 locker room, kept in spotless condition by our equipment manager Don Hewitt and a young staff. Tim Ryan, twenty-two, Eric Spies, twenty-one, Mark Coniglio, seventeen, Bob Messemer, twenty, Bobby Dominguez, seventeen, and Gerry Atkins, thirteen. They have been with us all summer, keeping us in uniforms, socks, jocks, T-shirts, towels. They lived right along with us at Fullerton from July to September, got room and board and nominal wages. Some of them have to go back to school and won't be around much during the week, but I'm sure we'll see all of them on game days, when each of them will have responsibilities at the Coliseum.

Gary Tuthill, George Menefee, and Garrett Giemont, our trainers, have their facilities here, too: taping tables, whirlpool baths, diathermy machines, ultrasound, cupboards full of tape and benzoin and plaster of paris and a lot of other stuff I'd rather not know about.

Our lockers aren't your usual kind of shower room gray steel locker: they're large open cages. After practice we hang up our pads and toss our T-shirts, socks and jocks into painted circles on the floor. Don Hewitt turns on big hot blowers to dry out the pads and after we leave he will do the laundry, so that each day we start with clean, dry things.

Alongside the field, just north of the north goal posts, we

hold our meetings in some little cinder-block buildings built by the Rams. They're nothing more or less than classrooms with chairs, chalkboards, movie screens, projectors and whole walls filled with cans of film. We watch a lot of film. We watch ourselves. We watch our opponents. And then, before we go home at night, our coaches might hand some of us a reel or two for us to watch, individually, at home. Each Ram has his own projector. I'm borrowing one until I get mine.

September 8

"ALL RIGHT," SAID KENNY MYER TODAY AT OUR NINE A.M. quarterback meeting. "Our league opener against Atlanta will not be any pushover for us. They're only two and four for the preseason. But they won their last two games, against Green Bay and Baltimore, and Steve Bartkowski, their quarterback, is sound again. The game will be in Atlanta and they have rabid fans there who will make it mighty tough on us if the Falcons jump out to an early lead." Kenny grew up in the South, and I swear that during this week's work on the Atlanta game, his accent is thickening a bit.

"They had success in the preseason," Kenny continued, "with a three-four defense—only three down linemen and four linebackers—something we didn't see a great deal of. So we have to work against that alignment. They'll also go into a three-three from time to time, with an extra defensive back, and when they do that, Ron will have to be ready with a selection of audibles, some runs, some passes, depending on the down and the distance."

Kenny looked up at me. "Naturally, Pat, you'll have to be

ready, too. Shack can't play with a broken thumb. Now, here's what we think we can do to Atlanta."

Almost everything Kenny had to say—and more—was in the play books he handed to each of us. Kenny—and all the other coaches—had spent hours on them, and they contained everything any of us could possibly want to know about Atlanta, names and numbers and even pictures of all their players, descriptions of the strengths and weaknesses, computer analyses of their defensive and offensive tendencies, their different defensive fronts, their overshifts and undershifts and four-threes and what pass coverages went with each of them. Sometimes, Kenny told me the other day, he comes to work at six A.M. on the days we get our play books. I believe it.

September 12

IT WAS A BRIGHT SUNNY DAY IN ATLANTA, 73 DEGREES, windless. But all the early bounces went the wrong way. Jim Bertelsen lost a couple of punts in the sun, Larry McCutcheon forgot to fall on a bobbled pitch, Dennis Harrah was illegally downfield on a shovel pass play that gained quite a few yards, Tom Dempsey dubbed a placement, and Ron Jaworski's last pass of the half was intercepted as the gun sounded. We trooped into the dressing room hanging our heads. We were down 7-6 and we weren't proud of ourselves.

We had run up 207 yards to Atlanta's 88, but we just seemed to sputter along. Our lone TD came on a scrambling roll-out pass from Ron to Harold Jackson in the end zone; Harold was so close to the end line one official ruled him out of bounds. All things considered, we were lucky we were only behind by one point. I couldn't help but wonder: if Jaworski doesn't put some points on the board, will they go with me? My more conservative self answered: "If Ron can't, why would they think *you* could?"

Coach Knox wasn't worried. "These guys aren't beating us. We're beating ourselves," he said. "Let's just not give up the ball anymore, huh? There's no reason why we can't go out and get us some points."

The offense came out strong. Taking over on our own 25, Jaworski ran Cappelletti to the left, McCutcheon to the right and then hit Harold Jackson on a strike over the middle to the Atlanta 43. All through the first half the Atlanta fans had rumbled and roared. Now they quieted down as Cappelletti and McCutcheon ran left, middle and right on seven consecutive running plays to the Atlanta one. No mistakes, no fumbles, no penalties. Then, on second and one, Ron kept the ball and dived over the top for a score: 12–7, Rams.

Shack and I were all over Ron on the sideline. "Way to go, Ron. Now that was something like it." Dempsey made the point-after-TD. But Ron was rubbing his right arm. "Feels numb," he said. He went behind the bench and started throwing the ball while the defense put the quietus on Bartkowski again; they had to punt and Ron trotted back in with a play from Kenny Myer: pitchout left to McCutcheon. Only trouble was, Ron had a hard time handling the ball. He had to pitch it out with his left hand and "Clutch" McCutcheon, who slowed up for the toss, was held to *nada*. "I can't feel a thing in my right arm," Ron said with a grimace at the sideline. His face was white.

All of a sudden, I was trotting out on the field. I don't remember who told me to go. Who else was there to go in as QB anyway? We ran off a couple of plays, exchanged punts with Atlanta and got the ball again on our 43. On three straight runs, we picked up a first down. First and ten on the Atlanta

47. Kenny sent in a sweep to McCutcheon. All of a sudden I realized: They're not going to let me pass at all. They don't trust the rookie. But then as we came up to the line of scrimmage, I noted Atlanta shifting into a three-three. Well now, I thought, I can call an audible. Sure enough, as I hunched down over center, I picked up the double coverage on Harold Jackson, single coverage on Jessie. "Two sixty-five," I shouted. "Two sixty-five." "Two" was the snap count I had called in the huddle. Saying it at this point meant I was changing the call. "Sixty-five" was the code number this week for a long pass to Jessie right under the goal post. If the guys only pick this up, I prayed, and give me just a little time— "Hike! Hike!" I faded back, glanced at Jackson, evaded the onrushing Claude Humphrey and saw that Ron had beaten his man. I let it go. The pass went 56 yards in the air. It wasn't picture-perfect and Jessie wasn't alone down there as I thought he'd be: their strong safety had faded back with him. But Jessie went up for it. And Jessie came down with it. In the end zone for six. My first pass in the NFL, a bomb for a touchdown!

I slapped hands with everyone but the men in the zebra shirts. I was taking some kind of chance out there, calling that audible. It would have been easier (and safer) not to call it. I could have said later that I just didn't see the new coverage, run the ball and if we didn't make the first down, why, just kick it and let the defense make the breaks. But no risk, no gain. I wanted to risk.

Dempsey converted. The score was 20–7. Shack Harris was telling me, over on the sidelines, that I'd made a gutsy call. Coach Knox came over and said, with just a trace of a smile, "We'd have preferred to see you run the ball, Pat, but under the circumstances . . ." I didn't smile at all. "O.K., Coach," I said, words that could have meant anything. But I wanted to tell Knox, "You said I was just a rookie, that I

51

didn't have any experience. But, shoot, I've had a lot of experience under pressure and I wasn't as nervous as some of the guys who were telling me not to get nervous."

The rest of the game was a blur to me. The coaches didn't ask me to throw another pass and I didn't call any more audibles. I saw a chance one more time, but I didn't want to press my luck. I'd be one for one on my first day in the NFL. Keeping the ball on the ground and playing for the breaks, we scored another TD (on an interception by Monte Jackson) and a field goal by Tom Dempsey. A 50-yard bomb from Bartkowski to Bubba Bean late in the fourth quarter mattered not a whit. We won, 30–14.

And the writers swarmed over me in the locker room. "I'm so lucky," I told the press. "It wasn't even a very good pass." But it had won the game. Carroll Rosenbloom stood off on the side, beaming. "He reminds me so much of John Unitas," said C.R. to anybody who'd listen to him. "He's so cool, he'd make the ice in Iceland melt," said Don Klosterman. "We weren't worried about Pat Haden," said Coach Knox. "Pat Haden can do the job."

I wonder if Coach Knox really thinks I can.

Steve Rosenbloom came over and sat with me for the last half of our flight. He is the owner's son and he oversees the business end of the operation, but he certainly doesn't put on any airs. Steve is thirty-one, has spent half his life working on a pro football team and the other half racing motorcycles while getting a degree at Georgetown U. He introduced himself to his wife-to-be by biting her in the arm in a Georgetown bar.

We had a philosophical discussion, about life and love and fate. "What kind of life would I be leading," he said, "if I'd been born to a laborer in Calcutta?" We agreed that he certainly wouldn't be jetting his way across the continent in the Rams' private plane. And neither would I.

So what? Well, Steve and I both think that since we have received a lot—due to no merit of our own—we have an obligation to give it back, somehow, some way. To God? Well, not directly. But to poor people, any people, whom we might, someday, be able to help.

September 13

BUMPS AND BRUISES AT BLAIR FIELD AT 12:30 P.M. UNLIKE many teams, we have no day off after a game. We check our injuries with the team trainers and doctors, we watch movies of the previous day's game, we have a light workout and then a little team party. Then we take our day off on Tuesday.

Today, our worst fears were confirmed on Ron Jaworski. He suffered the same injury Shack had last year: a broken rotator cuff in the right shoulder, something that makes throwing the ball next to impossible. Ron may be out for weeks. And Shack's thumb is still in a splint. I hate for it to happen this way, but now I have my big chance (as I knew I would, except that it's coming a lot sooner than I'd dreamed). I will probably start against Minnesota, a team that's one of the favorites, along with the Rams and Dallas, to go to the Super Bowl. In Bloomington, Minnesota, where they say the Rams never win.

Well, I'll show 'em.

September 14

ON MY DAY OFF, MY PHONE HARDLY STOPPED RINGING.
The Associated Press wants to take my picture. Maybe they
think I look different now that I'm a starting Ram quarterback. Mostly the calls were from members of the press,
wondering how I felt about starting against Minnesota. My
answers began to sound memorized. "Look, *any* quarterback
can look good with the Rams. Our defense is so good. We
run the ball so well. . . . I'm the toast of the town today,
but if I don't produce next week, I might find myself on the
next plane to Saskatchewan. . . . All I can do when the opportunity presents itself is put my best foot forward. . . .
But, hey, Shack's thumb could heal this week. . . ."

I am disappointed in most sports journalism. The questions
are always the same. My mind goes numb after a while. And
my answers tend to start sounding the same, too.

Cindy went to Palm Springs yesterday with her sister to
soak up some sun and I was just as glad she did. I actually
preferred to be by myself this week, before Minnesota. I am
nervous and preoccupied and Cindy is a girl who needs a lot
of attention. But barely an hour ago, Cindy phoned from
Palm Springs. It is cold and stormy there and she says she's
coming home today. And I really did want to be alone. Oh
well. I went out to one of those custom T-shirt places and
had a shirt made for her: I NEED ATTENTION. She'll wear it,
but it's actually for me, something to remind *me,* I've got a
wife who needs me.

I have a hundred reasons why I married Cindy. I love her.
She loves me. But we aren't much alike. Maybe that's what's
good about our being together. She helps me put my life into

some perspective. I'm uptight, she's hangloose. I'm literally *living* football these days. She doesn't give a hoot about athletics. She doesn't even come to some games.

September 15

THE GAME PLAN FOR MINNESOTA? COACH KNOX SAYS WE'RE going to run the ball down their throats. They were the biggest winners in the NFL on Sunday, beating New Orleans 40–9. But we think we can run on them. We'll run right at Eller, Sutherland, Page and Marshall. Gosh, I've been watching these guys since I was in grammar school.

Of course, Tarkenton is a real pro. He calls his own plays, he makes up his own plays in the huddle, and he is capable of putting up twenty-eight points against our defense. If that happens, it might change our game plan a bit. Then we'd have to open up. We're putting in four or five audibles, some runs, some short passes. Their defensive backs play conservatively, so we might be able to throw under their coverage. And we may use some trick plays: some reverses, a statue of liberty, a triple handoff pass.

But I won't have to make the decisions to call those. I'll be under enough pressure. The coaches will call the plays. I can understand that. This game may have some importance when the end of the season rolls around. And I wouldn't want some twenty-three-year-old kid calling the plays with my job in his hands. Someday, if I last long enough, I'll handle my own calls. The game is not that difficult. I have intelligence. I have courage. There is no reason why I can't contribute. The better quarterbacks do it anyway. Bradshaw, Tarkenton, Hart, Landry, Kilmer, Stabler.

September 17

BLOOMINGTON, MINNESOTA. THE REGISTRY HOTEL STICKS up along the freeway like a grain elevator. Metropolitan Stadium, just down the street and across a big parking lot, looks like a giant Erector set. It's a baseball stadium, and our visitors' dressing room was obviously designed for about twenty-five Tigers, not forty-three Rams. Awfully cramped—and the walls are covered with banners of all the teams in the American League: White Sox, Yankees, Red Sox, Indians. . . .

Papers say tomorrow's game is a sellout. The Rams have always given the Vikes a good game here and we're natural rivals. But, if you go on the record, you'd have to expect Minnesota to win. The Rams have only won once since they've been playing here and, with a rookie starting at quarterback against the great Tarkenton, we're 5½-point underdogs. But I say that we aren't the Rams who lost nine previous games here. Those Rams had names like Gabriel and Munson and Clancy Williams. Statistically-minded sportswriters don't always realize this: each year's team is different from the previous year's team. Sometimes radically different.

September 19

AFTER FIVE QUARTERS OF PLAY IN BLOOMINGTON, WE walked off the field with a 10–10 tie. Most football teams aren't a bit pleased with a tie. But we were almost elated.

56

We had outplayed a Super Bowl contender with one arm (mine!) tied behind our backs for most of the game and with any luck we would have won with a chip shot field goal in overtime. Before this game we weren't sure how good we really were. Now we have a sneaking suspicion that we are damned good.

Saying nothing in the tunnel, we trooped into the little visitors' dressing room. I grabbed a Coke from a refrigerator near the door and sat down in front of my cubicle and started ripping off my pads. Tom Dempsey, on my right, was shaking his head. Shack Harris, on my left, said, "We shoulda won it, but we were lucky not to lose it."

Then Coach Knox and his staff walked in. "Let's say a prayer," said Knox, speaking from a well of neon light in the middle of the room. I could hear him but I couldn't see him because there was a pillar right in my way with a sign on it that said HELP KEEP THIS PLACE CLEAN and another that told of dire penalties from the NFL if any of us were caught gambling or even talking to gamblers. Knox led us in the "Our Father."

Then he spoke. "I've never been prouder of a team in my life," he said. "Both teams played well enough to win. There were damn few penalties. This is how football should be played. It's probably the best game I ever saw." That was all. Knox is a man of few words. Then the coaches started circulating, each of them wanting to talk to their own special charges. Kenny Myer came right over to me. "You played the best game I ever saw a young quarterback play, Pat." I nodded and said we should have won. I said it again when Carroll Rosenbloom came by. "Sorry," I said, looking up at him. "We should have won it."

"Don't worry, kid," he said with warmth and a fine smile on his face. "You were great. With any kind of breaks, we could have won thirty-five to ten."

I looked up at him. He was serious and, by God, I believe he was right. I wanted to see a play-by-play right away. I wanted to review the entire game, alone with myself on the plane. But first I had to answer questions from the press. I had to go on the air with Dick Enberg from L.A.'s radio station KMPC. And then the reporters, some regulars, some new faces, had a thousand questions for me. Rich Roberts of the Long Beach *Press Telegram*. Bob Cox of the South Bay *Breeze*. Mitch Chortkoff of the Santa Monica *Outlook*. Doug Krikorian of the *Herald-Examiner*. Ross Newhan of the L.A. *Times*. They all seemed pleased. It was a helluva game. I don't know that I ever enjoyed a game more. And I'm sure these reporters not only loved the game, they took some delight in talking to those of us who had displayed some grace under pressure.

Some guy I didn't know—maybe he was a Minnesota writer—asked me about my height. "What about it?" I snapped. He stuttered and wondered whether maybe that wasn't trouble. "Look," I said, "in eight weeks of training camp and two games, out of maybe four or five hundred passes I've thrown, I have had two of them tipped. I'm as tall as Fran Tarkenton or Bob Berry or Bob Griese. But nobody ever asks Tarkenton how tall he is because he's been around sixteen years and he's done it. But you know, you don't throw with your height, you throw with your mind and your feet. You don't throw *over* these guys, you throw past 'em and between 'em." And I knew that when I did throw today, I threw well. I had to throw a couple away under a heavy rush. But I only got sacked once. And I completed some dandy passes.

On the plane they handed out Coors and hamburgers and I found a seat near the window, got a copy of the mimeographed play-by-play and plopped myself down to review what happened. The others who were filing in seemed happy, too happy to suit me, after a game we should have won. What kind of a team was this, I wondered, that is happy after a tie? Maybe the players are simply reflecting the feelings of Coach Knox, who plays mainly to "not lose." For me, that is not good enough.

Hell, we started out like gangbusters, breaking through huge gaps in Minnesota's front, tearing right by Alan Page and Jim Marshall, the down linemen on their right side. The sod was sloppy; that made it harder for McCutcheon to run his favorite sweeps. But it didn't matter. On our second possession, starting on our own 24, we 10-yarded them to death and drove right down to their 1-yard line.

Fourth and goal on the one. What now? Kick a field goal and get something on the board? I was surprised when Chuck Knox didn't do that. And delighted. Hell, we marched 75 yards. I knew we could get one more. Cappelletti over left tackle? Why not? The reason why not was that the Vikes were ready. And able to stop this particular thrust.

We came off the field with Vikings' applause ringing in our ears: they *had* done a good job stopping us. But we had done a good job running through them. There wasn't a doubt in my mind that we could run on them all day. But oh Lordy, if we could run like this, we should have been able to pass occasionally, too. Passes work best when you don't *have* to pass. "We can pass against these guys," I had told Kenny Myer on the sideline.

"I know, kid, I know," he said.

We got the ball back at midfield and Kenny did have me passing. On second and eight, I hit McCutcheon over the middle for a 20-yard gain to the Viking 34, Cappelletti broke a tackle and gained 7 on a great second effort and then I got the wig-wag for a roll-out pass to the right. It was a play where Cappelletti could pick his own spot, fake the linebacker one way and go the other. He made a good fake on

Matt Blair and Blair started to slip, so I threw an easy toss to John as he headed toward the sideline. But Blair recovered, got to his feet and went high in the air for the interception. That hurt. Not so much because it gave the Vikes good field position (which they used to get Fred Cox lined up for a 33-yard field goal) but because it shook my coaches' confidence in my passing.

Myer was trying to be cool on the sideline but having a hard time of it. "Did you see the tight end?" he demanded. "You see him? He was clear." I nodded. I wasn't bothered by the interception. John Cappelletti was clear too. Matt Blair, a super athlete, just made a very good play, that's all. It wasn't the end of the world. And it wouldn't destroy *my* confidence. I wasn't so sure about Kenny and Chuck.

But I was wrong. They sent in four more pass plays before the half ended. I completed two of them, both to McCutcheon, and scrambled on two of them under a heavy rush, gaining 4 yards on one scramble and throwing the ball away on another.

After the half, with the score 0–3, there was little doubt in my mind that we could beat Minnesota. After three quarters of play, with the score still 0–3, there was still no doubt in my mind. We were moving the ball well, had kept it, in fact, for the last seven minutes of the third quarter, and were on the Viking 25. Moments later I found Harold Jackson getting clear in the end zone and fired for him. It was overthrown, but the officials called Nate Allen for interference and we had the ball on the Viking's 1-yard line, first down.

"O.K.," I said in the huddle, "this is it. Four downs to make one. Let's do it." We didn't do it. "Clutch" McCutcheon fumbled, Minnesota recovered and it was their ball, first and ten on their own 20. The breaks.

More breaks. Tarkenton, unable to run the ball, had to pass. Sensing this, we went into a blitz. Trouble was, Tark put up a long one to Sammie White, Rod Perry slipped and fell, and all of a sudden we were down 10–0.

Not good, being ten points down to the Vikes in the fourth quarter. But that was precisely what we needed to get us going.

Now we couldn't just lie back and play our cautious, waiting, opportunistic game. We had to go on the attack. And we did. From our own 28, on four runs and five passes, we moved 48 yards to the Viking 24, where we bogged down. But we got points this time: Dempsey kicked a field goal from there to make it 3–10.

We held them. They held us. Then our break. Rod Perry redeemed himself for his earlier fall in the open field by stripping the ball from Brent McClanahan at the Viking 36 and running it to the 11, where Chuck Foreman knocked him out of bounds.

Our first down on the 11. What to do? Leeman Bennett figured the Vikings were guessing we would run. He sent in a pass, a sideline to Harold Jackson, and I was glad. I took the snap, stepped back and zipped it toward the flag, Harold gobbled it in and went out of bounds on the 1. First down, again, on the 1. Again: four downs to make one. Would we do it this time? Yes, but barely. Cappelletti was stopped twice over left guard. Jim Bertelsen came in for John with the same damn play. "C'mon you guys, this is it," I said. "Fire out." They did, Bert went up and over and into the end zone: 9–10! Demps made the automatic point-after-TD and it was a new ball game, 10–10.

Two minutes left. Could either of us break the tie? Nope. Now we were in sudden death overtime. First score wins. Vikings won the toss and elected to receive. That turned out O.K., because it gave us the wind at our backs, which could have helped. But not so you could tell from Dempsey's kickoff; he booted it short to the Viking 10 and then Sammie White returned it 36 big yards to the Viking 46. That was when

Tark put the ball deep, deep enough for Monte Jackson to pick it off and give us our chance from the 16.

We grabbed at that chance and moved the ball up-field—as we had all day. Cappelletti and McCutcheon gained 5 between them, I passed to John for 7 and a first down, then threw another to Ron Jessie, good for 21 yards to midfield. Then, working deliberately so we wouldn't give up the ball, we ran right over these guys. Clutch picked up 40 yards on four straight carries to the Viking 19, Cappelletti and Clutch picked up 6 more and, on fourth down and four, Tom Dempsey came in for the automatic field goal. He missed it. We'll have to look at the films to see what happened. But Nate Allen got a hand on it, it rolled into the end zone and the Vikings had another chance.

What a ball game. We exchanged punts. Then Tarkenton drove the Vikes, passing to Foreman and Voigt and scrambling himself, all the way down to our 11. Shoot! Now the Vikes were in field goal range.

But Tarkenton faltered there. He passed for Sammie White at the goal line and Rick Kay went up high in the air, grabbed it and tumbled back into the end zone for a touchback. Another chance for us. 1:04 left in overtime. Time enough. But no! The officials didn't give us the touchback, didn't put the ball on the 20 as the NFL's "impetus" rule seemed to dictate. They placed it on the 1! That did it. That killed us, because there on the 1, we had no opportunity to win it, we just had to try and not lose it. We had to play it safe. I fell on the ball for no gain. I fell on the ball again for a gain of 2. The Vikes took time out. I fell on the ball once more and the game was over.

September 20

T<small>ODAY'S REVIEWS WERE GOOD</small>. J<small>OHN</small> H<small>ALL OF THE</small> L.A. *Times*
wrote that "Pat Haden, in the clutch, made Francis Tarkenton
look a thousand years old." And Doug Krikorian of the
Herald-Examiner had this colorful assessment: "Clearly, the
Ram quarterback of the future has become the quarterback
of now after yesterday's impressive performance in which he
completed 11 of 22 passes for 136 yards and ran the Ram
offense as though he has been doing it for 10 years." Krikorian said that James Harris and Ron Jaworski might well
have something he called "a Wally Pipp feeling." Wally Pipp
was the guy who got sick one day to be replaced by a young-
ster named Gehrig and never returned to the Yankee lineup.

Of course, that's just newspaper talk. I think Harris will
probably be starting against the New York Giants next Sunday.
NFL Properties may be impressed enough to call (as they
did this morning) to negotiate the rights to a Pat Haden poster.
But that's show biz. Knox isn't going to give the starting job
to a rookie.

Krikorian has been talking about "the great QB debate"
but there isn't any debate where it counts, in the coaches'
room. Harris is simply number one, period. And Ron Jaworski is number two. Or, as Bob Cox of the South Bay
Daily Breeze put it a month ago, "Pat Haden is destined to be
a telephone operator this season, relaying messages from assistant coaches high above the stadium."

I went to Blair Field early today to get some treatment for
my calf. I must have gotten kicked there yesterday; could
hardly walk on it this morning. But Gary Tuthill did some

magic: he shot some electricity through the calf that made the muscles expand and contract and applied ultrasound and made me sit in a cold whirlpool bath for a while and after that I was definitely O.K. Tut is a wonder, a husky guy (like most of the trainers I've ever known) who was my trainer for a time at USC and now puts in about twelve hours a day for the Rams. He likes the Rams so much he has undertaken to manage our so-called basketball team during the off-season. Two or three nights a week he assembles anywhere from five to twelve of the Rams who like basketball to play various church and club groups around Southern California, generally as part of some fund-raiser. Jessie and Jackson and Simpson are the best players. But even a hulk like Doug France will get into the act.

We all looked at the game movies together, but they didn't tell us much we didn't know already. The snap from center on our fifth-quarter field goal attempt was a little high; it gave Nate Allen two-tenths of a second more to get to the ball—and that was all he needed.

Tonight my old college gang and I got together at Joe Collins' place in Hermosa for "Monday Night Football." Stabler made a monkey out of Kansas City's rookie corner-back for a while, but the kid hung in there and made a nice interception toward the end of the game. Each of us put five dollars in a total point pool, I picked forty-two and came close enough to win. I am just lucky. In almost everything. Tonight I found a parking place right in front of my apartment, a spot where none of my visitors can ever find a parking stall closer than three or four hundred yards.

September 21

JOE COLLINS CAME TO OUR HOUSE FOR DINNER. HE WAS really up: he's just gotten a job as a time salesman for KNX Radio. It's a good job, and he had to fight for it for more than a year. I knew he would get it. He is a real competitor, a guy who took his Loyola High team to the CIF Playoffs two years in a row and, without a great deal of natural talent, made the varsity for three years at SC.

John McKay phoned us from Tampa. He isn't very happy there. Spurrier isn't having a very good season; John manages to get open a lot but Spurrier's not throwing him the ball and, most importantly, the team's not winning. Nobody expected them to win much, but when you've won all your life . . .

September 22

WE GOT OUR SPECIAL PLAY BOOK ON THE GIANTS TODAY. And Shack took over the number one group. But I still have to be ready. Kenny Myer came over to me quietly and said, "Hang in there, Pat, anything can happen."

I brought home some reels of New York Giants' defense in three recent games. We have technicians who break down game films—so our offense looks only at their defense. And our defense sees only their offense. As I studied the Giants' defense, it seemed to me as if Clyde Powers, the Giants' strong safety, was tipping the coverage. When it's a zone, he turns and faces the quarterback; if he faces the slot man, it's man to man. That is an important tip for our quarterback: if he knows they're in a man-for-man, his job is easier by a half. I'll have to tell Shack at breakfast in the morning. This may help us. Then again, it may not. I wonder if the Giants themselves always know what coverage they're in. I'm afraid of teams like this; they're up and down and unpredictable as hell.

September 25

ON THE EVE OF EVERY HOME GAME WE CHECK INTO THE Beverly Hilton Hotel, attend a team meeting at nine and a hamburger buffet at ten. We're expected to be in bed, with the lights out, at eleven. The assistant coaches come around to make sure. And on some of the guys, they'll check twice.

This is mainly to protect us against ourselves. If we stayed home the night before a game, we'd be besieged with dinner invitations, one after-dinner drink could lead to another, and we'd be in no shape for any contest on Sunday.

September 26

SUNDAY. I HADN'T BOTHERED READING THE PAPER THIS morning, just attended the Rams chapel service, ate breakfast, sat in on the team meeting and drove slowly down Wilshire Boulevard toward the Coliseum. When I got to the dressing room, Shack was there with a copy of the L.A. *Times* in his hand. He had a mournful expression on his face and said, "I'm sorry about this, Pat. I didn't say all this stuff. This guy got the story all wrong." He handed me the paper.

Across the bottom of page one was a feature by Skip Bayless: "HARRIS CAN'T ESCAPE POCKET OF PREJUDICE." I read it quickly, almost four full columns of print. It was the fruit, apparently, of an interview Shack had had this week with the reporter, who was obviously trying to do a story that the regular pro football reporters had been successfully avoiding for more than two years now. It was more sociology than sport, a story that tried to answer the question: What is it like to be the first black quarterback to make it big in the NFL? According to this story, it isn't much fun for Harris because people-at-large—the indeterminate "they"—do not accept him as a pro quarterback. His proof? He was getting "a bad press."

I thought to myself, actually, Harris is getting press notices that are no worse than most quarterbacks get in the NFL. Pro football fans, the press included, give quarterbacks too much blame in defeat. And of all the twenty-eight quarterbacks in the league, only the guy who ends up winning the Super Bowl doesn't end up being called a loser.

But in this piece, Shack was saying he was getting a bad press *because he was black:* "I'm just not as accepted by the press because I'm a black quarterback." Maybe that was true. Maybe it wasn't. But I could see where Shack might find some justification for thinking it was. Historically, blacks had had to struggle for acceptance in the sports world, most notably in baseball, tennis and golf. In pro football, too. In the beginning, or at least starting in the 1930's, pro football was a game for whites. Gradually, the barriers came down. They had to. What coach wouldn't play a black kid with burning speed at wide receiver or corner back? Gradually, as more and more blacks went to college and became very skilled at every position, they fit in anywhere.

Except at quarterback. Quarterback was something special. Lots of blacks had made it as quarterbacks in college. Few did so in the pros. Why? The only real answer has to be that they weren't good enough. Damn few college quarterbacks of *any* color make it in the pros. But the pseudoanswers abounded. "Blacks don't have the brains for it." Or, if they do have the brains, if they are whip-smart, all-A students with Phi Beta Kappa keys, then: "They don't have the heart."

I thought Shack had destroyed this shibboleth. To the people who counted, he had proven he could do the job. To himself. To his teammates. To the Ram coaches. Who else mattered? (Shack had had a helluva time in his earlier incarnation as quarterback for the Buffalo Bills, a four-year stretch when he knew he wasn't number one in the hearts of the Buffalo fans and never was sure where he stood in the assessments of the Buffalo coaches either. But in L.A. he quickly won the job over the veteran John Hadl and as soon as he did, the Rams traded Hadl to Green Bay, and right in the middle of the 1974 season at that!) I'd seen Shack at work, close up now for eleven weeks. I knew he was a very good quarterback, and, as self-confident as I was, I had reconciled myself to playing behind him, for this season at least. Rookies *never* make it at quarterback on a playoff contender. And anyway, I only had to look at the statistics from the NFL office. Shack was leading all the quarterbacks in both leagues. He'd completed thirty of forty-six passes for 494 yards, 65 percent, and had an efficiency rating of 121. Ken Anderson led the NFL last year with 95.9.

But this newspaper piece had Shack saying this wasn't enough. He wanted—*publicity?* That's what he seemed to be saying: "I don't mind competing for the job. But with the publicity I get, how can I keep it? Yes, Ron and Pat do get better publicity . . . because they're white."

After I read the piece I said, "It's O.K., Shack. I understand."

I could understand how Shack might believe that I *was* getting a better press. I probably was. L.A. writers have always seemed to be overly kind, overly protective and overly biased for me and to me. There were a lot of reasons for that. I was a local boy, I'd proven my ability in high school championship games and had been a part of three Pac-8 championship teams at SC and dazzled the WFL through most of a season at the Southern California Sun. The fact that I was white could only be of significance to a black who has been conditioned to think of his blackness and therefore, the odds against him, step-by-cussed-step of the way up the ladder of success. (I do not blame him: it is part of being talented and black in America. But where have I been all of these years? It is only now that I begin to realize the height and the depth and the breadth of racism in this country—and what it has done and is doing to my black brother, Shack.)

The thing that I did not understand, however, was Shack's saying that his "bad press" threatened his position as number one: "I don't mind competing for the job. But with the publicity I get, how can I keep it?" What does he mean by this? Standing there getting ready for the Giant game, of course, was not the time to try and find out. Shack was starting today, after a three-game layoff, and he needed all the concentration he could muster for this game. I let it go, we suited up and went out to warm up.

And, naturally enough, after that layoff, Shack's timing was a little off. On his first series the Rams went nowhere and the Giants promptly drove the length of the field for a field goal. On the second series he was intercepted on our 33-yard line, booed badly as he came off the field, and booed again when he came on again (for the Giants had scored after that interception on a pass from Craig Morton to Bob Tucker, to make the score 0–10). Only on Shack's third series did he get in the groove. Then he passed smartly to Harold Jackson and Bob Klein to set up a 10-yard touchdown run by John Cappelletti.

We ended up winning, 24–10, and Shack's stats looked good: 14 for 23 and 179 yards. But only rarely did the offense look sharp. The Giants were taking away our sweeps, stacking the outside and bringing their backs up way too fast, daring us to pass and finding that we dared too seldom. Again, however, our general, play-it-safe-and-wait-for-the-breaks strategy paid off. The defense got us the ball on the Giant 35; Cappelletti took it in from there on a beautiful run after a swing pass from Harris. Midway through the fourth quarter, Butch Robertson intercepted a Morton pass to give us the ball on the Giant 9, and three plays later, Bertelsen plunged in for our final score.

The Giants were a lot better than we'd been led to believe and hurt us in more ways than one. Tackle Merlin Olsen pulled a hamstring and Linebacker Rick Kay is out for the season with a wrecked knee. Mike Fanning went in for Ole and did a great job, stopping Larry Csonka on fourth and one at our 22 when the score was still tied in the third quarter. But Morton and Doug Kotar ran a lot at Kay's sub, Kevin McLain, and Jim Youngblood moved into that crucial spot at left linebacker.

I am sure I will be on the bench from now on, but I am glad I am not playing for New York. In the next four weeks they face St. Louis, Dallas, Minnesota and Pittsburgh—all of them playoff contenders. If they're still in the league after that, they should get a special team trophy.

October 3

MIAMI. I AM CONSTANTLY IMPRESSED WITH JAMES HARRIS, but today he bowled me over. Today, against Don Shula's Miami Dolphins, a team that reinvented modern pass defense, Shack threw twenty-nine times and completed seventeen picture passes for a total of 436 yards as we beat Miami, 31–28.

Time after time he hit Jessie, Jackson and McCutcheon, often when they were not primary receivers at all. On one 49-yard pass to Jackson with the score tied in the fourth quarter, Harold was a quaternary receiver—fourth choice! Another time, with the Rams trailing 14–21, third and seven at the Miami 15, Shack handed off to McCutcheon, who ran right, then wheeled and threw a one-bounce lateral back to him. Shack scooped it up and ran 12 yards to the Miami 3. We didn't plan for the lateral to bounce, but, as Shack told Clutch before the game, "I don't care if you toss it back on the ground, as long as I can reach it." And I was impressed by Harris' ability to overcome Miami's big lead. They were ahead 14–0 at the half. But we came back, under Shack's leadership, and we won.

This game ought to settle the Great Quarterback Controversy once and for all. It ought to settle another doubt as well. Critics have accused Coach Knox and his staff of being too conservative—and too bullheaded to change plans in the heat of battle. Well, it took the coaches a little while to adjust—mainly because the Dolphins came at us with a five-man line (which was a surprise—and an open dare for us to pass more than we liked to). We were stubborn. We're leading the conference in rushing. We want to establish the run, no matter what. But the coaches did change their thinking in the second quarter and Shack started throwing—with increasing effectiveness as the game wore on.

Thank God, they did and he did (and some beautiful passing it was, too). For some inexplicable reason, our defense had a terrible day, allowing the Dolphins to rack up 219 yards rushing and 100 passing. There are some guys on the team who haven't tackled Runner Benny Malone yet. But in the last two minutes, after we'd gone ahead on Tom Dempsey's 19-yard field goal (his fourth attempt of the afternoon), the defense came through. Dave Elmendorf and Bill Simpson each grabbed off one of Bob Griese's passes and that was that.

In the bedlam of the winner's locker room Carroll Rosenbloom, who enjoyed beating the coach who had run out on him at Baltimore, broke through the ring of reporters around Shack, whispered something in his ear and kissed him on the cheek. C.R. had beaten Shula and victory was sweeter than usual.

Coach Knox gave Don Hewitt, our equipment manager, a game ball today—for ingenuity above and beyond the call of duty. When we arrived at the stadium this morning, we found someone had broken into our locker room and made off with a dozen helmets. Somehow on a Sunday morning in Miami, Don managed to buy a few helmets, rebuild some extras he had and work out an involved system of trades between members of the offense and the defense (who weren't also members of the same special team).

Hewitt is a good man who keeps us and our equipment in excellent condition. He'd be perfect if he didn't keep bugging us every day of the week to "Sign the balls!" I think the Rams must give away (or sell) a couple hundred balls a week. And they always have to be signed by every member of the squad. A few signatures? O.K. But every time we turn around, there's Don shouting, "Sign the balls! Sign the balls!"

At this stage of my career I do not mind so much. It was only a few weeks ago, before I made the team, that Don was shouting, "Sign the balls! Sign the balls! Rookies *don't* sign 'em. Rookies *don't* sign 'em."

Flying back to L.A., Ron Jaworski and I had to laugh together over Coach Knox's pregame antics in the locker room. In his talk before the game Knox was full of fire, shouting that he wanted us to go out and "beat the bleep out of those bleepers." Then, without skipping a beat, he added quietly, "Let's say a prayer."

Coach Knox is a gentleman seven times over and a religious man as well. But this is a kind of war we are waging and we expect our general, no matter how religious he is, to talk in the tones of a soldier. In the locker room "beating the bleep out of 'em" is not unseemly talk. Ron and I imagine that Shula, also a religious man who goes to daily Mass and communion, speaks in the same obscene accents.

October 5

I SEE BY THE MORNING PAPER THAT NEW ENGLAND BEAT Oakland 48–17, rolling up 296 yards running and 172 yards on seventeen passes by Steve Grogan. This is the way Coach Knox likes to see the game played: establish the run, then pass when you *want* to, not when you *have* to. But the thing I liked best about the New England strategy (insofar as I can tell from the story in the L.A. *Times*): though the Patriots were ahead 21–10 at the half, they didn't sit on their lead against the fearsome Raiders. Instead, they kept rolling up the yards, on the land and in the air, and scored two touchdowns in each of the final quarters. Will the Rams ever do that? I doubt it. When we get ahead, we nurse it, punt a lot, and let the other team make the mistakes against our great defense. That'll usually work—except, like yesterday, on days when our defense breaks down or our kicking game goes bad.

Today, in practice, we worked out against a five-man line. Miami had success with it against us. We're afraid that the 49ers may try it too. If they do, we want to be ready.

October 6

CRITICS' CORNER. JIM MURPHY IN *Pro Football West:*

James Harris has given the ultimate demonstration that the perennial quarterback controversy is a dead issue. Jaworski and Haden are still around should Harris come down with another injury but that's the only way they will get him out of the lineup.

Harris is tired of all the talk about who is number one, and he's made his opinion known in interviews, thus adding fuel to the fire. But last Sunday in Miami he put the fire out the only way he could—with a devastating display of passing that silenced his detractors once and for all. James Harris is the quarterback.

October 7

TWO YOUNG MEN CAME TO SEE ME TONIGHT. THEY WERE reporters for the Birmingham High School paper in the San Fernando Valley. Some of the players don't like to give interviews to high school papers and maybe, someday, I won't either. But I haven't been out of high school that long myself. And I learn something in every interview.

The kids ended up staying to talk even after they'd finished asking a set of canned questions (and I'd finished giving them my canned answers). Celebrity interviews are too ritualized and reporters sometimes ask questions that give celebrities too much respect. An athlete's opinion on art or science or politics or religion doesn't deserve any kind of respectful attention—unless that athlete has some special expertise in one or another of those fields. Rudy Brutocao, a high school chum of mine, wants me to endorse his dad, who is running for the U.S. Congress out in West Covina. I have resisted. Why should anyone vote for Lou Brutocao just on my say-so? What do I know about the problems confronting the state this year? How do I know Lou Brutocao will do a better job than his opponent?

And now, here tonight, when I said to these young reporters that I might want to go into politics someday, one of them said, "I'd vote for you."

"You would?" I said. "You don't even know what I stand for."

He blinked. I was coming out of my preestablished role as high and mighty hero (who expected obeisance as a matter of course) and trying to establish some kind of thoughtful interchange. I was happy with his reaction. He turned off his tape recorder and we launched into a subject that interested him even more: himself, his future, his desire to go into broadcast journalism. I'd been talking to a lot of reporters over the past few years; coming out of that, I had some advice for him: "In any interview situation," I said, "forget your canned questions. Better to just carry on a good conversation. Listen to what I say. Your next question will come naturally enough. That question may not be in your notes. And asking it will take us off on a tangent. But sometimes you'll find more interesting things on one of these side trips than you will by following your prepared itinerary."

October 8

I DO NOT EXPECT TO PLAY AT ALL MONDAY NIGHT AGAINST the 49ers. It would make some sense to put me in there for the experience, so that if Harris does get hurt I'll be ready. As it is now, however, I have a feeling that I'll only play if: 1) we get way ahead, 2) Harris does poorly or 3) Harris gets hurt. So, if I'm in there, the odds are two to one that something has gone wrong. That's a weird feeling. I certainly don't want to root against anybody. I don't want to see James Harris do poorly or get hurt. But, on the other hand, I want to play.

I discussed all this with my dad yesterday. It was his birthday. I took him to lunch and we had a good chance to talk about my future with the Rams. The way I figure, James Harris is twenty-nine years old, he's at the prime of his career. What should I do? Maybe, after the season's over, I'll go to management and see what their plans are for me. Maybe I can get traded to Tampa. I could play there and make a lot more money. I've seen lots of other quarterbacks in the league. I'm as good as or better than many of them. So's Ron Jaworski.

On the other hand, maybe I won't have to find another place. Shack told me last week he didn't think he'd be around next year. He says management doesn't like him; he hears they've been talking to Joe Namath. Namath still wants to play in L.A.

October 11

IN FULL SIGHT OF GOD AND EVERYBODY, ON "MONDAY NIGHT Football," the 49ers beat us badly, 16–0. They put a frightening rush on Shack, sacked him ten times for losses of 97 yards and, on successive possessions in the third quarter, forced him to fumble twice—the first time on our 5-yard line and the second on our 14. San Francisco converted both breaks into scores and a 16–0 lead. By then, the way things were going, the game was already lost.

"The way things were going . . ." Our offensive line had been cited for holding penalties four times in the first quarter. They had to be too cautious after that. And then, when we got behind, the 49ers' defensemen just started swarming in on Harris. On one series in the fourth quarter, the Niners' front four sacked Harris on three straight plays for a loss of 31 yards.

Next to me in the locker room, Shack told the press, "I put too much pressure on our offensive line. I probably held the ball too long. I feel like I could have gotten the ball off quicker, and that would have helped."

October 12

THE *Times* SEEMED UNDULY CRUEL TO JAMES HARRIS THIS morning. On page one they ran a four-column photo of Harris going down under a rush by Tommy Hart and a three-column photo of Shack sitting down on the turf without the ball.

The *Times'* professorial expert on the Rams, Bob Oates, had some harsh words to go along with the pictures: "A large part of the reason for Harris' misfortune was his relative immobility when back to pass and his insistence on holding the ball too long instead of throwing it away. Against a heavy rush, the way to pass is fast . . . when Tarkenton faces a powerful front four, he either throws instantly or scrambles instantly. In this game, Harris did neither. Harris' other error was in failing to protect the ball when hit. It's one thing to lose 10 yards on a sack, but the worst thing is to lose the ball."

And Jim Murray of the *Times* was at his hyperbolic, hysterical best: "One 'sack' a game," he wrote, "is an embarrassment. Ten is Waterloo, Dunkirk, Little Big Horn, the Sack of Rome, the Visigoths at the gates. Anarchy."

October 14

BOB OATES HAD SOME SECOND THOUGHTS ABOUT OUR LOSS Monday night. We lost, he wrote, because the NFL told the officials to start cracking down, in this Monday-night showcase, on offensive holding. So the refs called us four times for holding in the first quarter. That, he said, ruined the momentum and tempo of the Ram offense. "The Rams weren't doing anything different Monday night, but the officials were . . . This was a game that turned on an NFL rules interpretation."

Our own coaches had some second thoughts, too: today they put in some screen passes—plays designed to take advantage of a swarming rush. Shack said he wondered why they didn't put these things in the play book *last* week: they knew San Francisco had a charging front four, didn't they?

His words had a bitter ring—and no wonder. His arm was in a sling today. On one of those horrible San Francisco sacks Shack hurt his shoulder again and Dr. Robert Kerlan, probably the best orthopedist in the sports world, told Shack he couldn't play for at least two weeks. Ron Jaworski's still hurting. So I'll probably start against the Chicago Bears on Sunday in the Coliseum. What a season!

Eight NFL quarterbacks have been knocked out of games this year—including Steve Bartkowski of Atlanta and Terry Bradshaw of Pittsburgh.

Naturally, I am prejudiced, but I think the league ought to take some steps to protect the quarterback, the most vulnerable man on the field.

The rulesmakers already know what they can do: they can impose stiffer penalties on rushers who hit late or pile on when the play is already stopped, maybe even eject them from the game. Al Davis and John Madden of the Raiders have proposed a passer be treated the same way a punter is—the moment his arm begins to move forward with the pass, he should be legally unhittable. And John Brodie, the 49er veteran QB, has suggested legalizing the intentional grounding of a forward pass. The question is: will they do any or all of these things? If they don't, quarterbacks will continue to drop. The game can't afford that loss.

October 15

I WENT TO A TROJAN CLUB MEETING TONIGHT AT O.B.'s Cellar, an SC hangout run by the O'Bradovich family. Steve and Jim, who went to Southern Cal with me, are both real good guys, and so is their dad, Bob.

Jon Arnett, one of the fleetest running backs in USC and Ram history (and now an executive talent scout in L.A.) is the president of this group and he gave me not only an introduction but an endorsement as well. He said I should have been starting for the Rams ever since my performance at Minnesota—and confided to my agent, Chuck Barnes, at the bar beforehand that he had said as much to Don Klosterman, the Rams' general manager, earlier in the week. I wonder how much lobbying like this goes on behind the scenes.

I told the group some jokes about J. K. McKay and me and our days at SC. Assistant Coach Craig Fertig had suggested that, academically speaking, we ought to start out kind of easy. So he enrolled us in Basketweaving One. First day we went into class and found only twelve in attendance—and they were all Navajo Indians. Worse, the instructor told us he graded on the curve.

And then I told the group I didn't know whether I'd start against the Bears. "The coaches make a policy," I said, "of not saying who's going to start at quarterback until right before a game. The theory is that if we don't know, we'll all prepare."

Somebody asked me if I would play for the Rams for ten years. I said I didn't know if I wanted to do that. "Not for a hundred thousand dollars a year?" he demanded.

"It's easy to make money," I said. The group laughed. They are a fairly affluent group and they laughed. But I really believe that I can. I'm just speaking from my own experience. Making money has always been easy for me. And I think it always will be. I like that feeling. It means that I can do what I *want* to do with my life, not what I *have* to do.

It was fun being with the Trojan Club. They were loud, boisterous, having fun, and most of their questions were not serious. "Is it true," someone asked me, "that you're taller than Jon Arnett?"

Jon answered that one: "When I started in the NFL," he said, "I was six four. Then I started running off tackle and—you can see what happened."

Later, in the bar, I had a couple of beers with two class-mates of mine, Joe Collins and John Nelson. We watched the wild ending of the last playoff game between Kansas City and the Yankees. But I didn't get as much of a chance as I wanted to talk to them: I spent most of my time at the bar fighting off the advances of a blonde who said she wanted to know me better. In a nice way, of course. One of the other perils—or pleasures—of being a quarterback in the NFL.

October 16

I WAS IN CHARGE OF THE OFFENSIVE MEETING AT THE Beverly Hilton tonight and it felt right to be doing that. There are certain kinds of passes I like to throw—68's and 62's, which are deep outs and deep curls—and I found Harold Jackson and Ron Jessie agreeing with me: they like me to throw them. I get the feeling that everyone is rallying around me and that our offense will put some early points on the board. So far, in five games, we have scored no points in the first quarter. We've fumbled too much—and at inopportune times.

We can't go on marching the length of the field and then give up the ball. We've got to start scoring early. If we do, I have a strong feeling that Jessie or Jackson—or both of them—will be the guys who help us do it.

To me, Jessie and Jackson are two of our real superstars. If it is true that we can score from anywhere on the field, it is only because of these two wide receivers. Both of them have been underrated (and still are in some quarters). Ron Jessie was a tested veteran with Detroit and only making $16,000 a year when he played out his option and signed with the Rams before the '75 season. Harold Jackson was originally drafted by the Rams and then Coach George Allen, wary of rookies, traded him to Philadelphia for a veteran who never did anything for the Rams. Four years later Harold came back as part of the trade that sent Roman Gabriel to the Eagles.

But Jessie and Jackson get the highest ratings from me. They are quiet guys; but they speak to me loud and clear when I see one or the other of them streaking down the field, a step or two ahead of a defender (and no free safety nearby). Then, my heart leaps and I fire. It is my biggest thrill in football. And probably the biggest thrill, too, for 99 percent of our fans.

October 17

THE RAM FANS APPLAUDED WHEN I RAN ONTO THE FIELD today and it was a loud, rather-more-sustained applause that had an unmistakable meaning: there were a lot of Angelenos who were glad to see me taking over. The reason, I think, is part of an American myth that has nothing whatever to do with football—and everything to do with what goes on in the minds of football fans. Melvin Durslag of the *Examiner* alluded to it this week when he described me as "the prototype of the quarterback Alex Karras used to hate. This is the sort, complained Alex, who gets the breakfast-food commercial while Greeks and Italians in the middle of the line get the ones selling ointment to clear up acne."

I tried not to disappoint the fans: after Cullen Bryant returned the opening kickoff to our 28, I marched the Rams all the way down to the Bear 28. And then Larry McCutcheon fumbled. I did not fault Clutch. The Bears were hitting awfully hard and I wasn't sure Clutch would come out of this game alive.

But we were hitting hard, too. We held the Bears on downs, they punted and we started another drive from midfield. "C'mon you guys," I said when I ducked into the huddle. "We gotta win this one or we aren't gonna have any fun at Mack's party tonight." Doug France frowned and growled that I should get serious. I was serious. This was my big chance. But I believe we all play better when we're loose, even laughing.

This time we drove to the Bears' 18, then had to settle for a field goal when I was sacked under a safety blitz—which I should have seen coming and didn't—on third and thirteen.

But our defense got us the ball back almost immediately: Fred Dryer forced Walter Payton to fumble at the Bear 17 and Jim Youngblood recovered. I sent McCutcheon around end for a short gain, then passed to Clutch, who was wide open on the goal line: 10–0, Rams. We were scoring points. And in the first quarter at that.

That's about as much as I remember of the game. On our next possession I faded to pass on third and six, then scrambled under a heavy rush and thought I could get a first down when I saw daylight to my left. I found darkness. Later they told me that Wally Chambers and Waymond Bryant, 250 and 239 pounds respectively, had caught me in a vise and crunched me down on our 25-yard line. They also told me I didn't move for a full two minutes. When play resumed, I was on the bench, too groggy even to spell Rhodes.

October 18

Ron Jaworski throws a hard ball: according to the papers this morning our receivers dropped the first three passes Ron attempted, passes that could have scored or led to scores. The Bears went ahead 12–10 on some fine passing by Bob Avellini and some pretty running by the second-year sensation, Walter Payton. Then Ron came through with a pair of long passes to Ron Jessie in the fourth quarter. Both of them set up scores and we won 20–12.

I still have a headache. Dr. Kerlan says I suffered a slight concussion and that scares me. I had two concussions at Bishop Amat, one at SC and one last year with the Sun. How many concussions can a guy take before he starts to lose his marbles?

But I am more angry than scared. The Bear game was a big opportunity for me. I was doing well and, if I'd stayed in the game, I would have done better. I was planning to start against New Orleans this coming Sunday and, after these two starts, I don't really think anyone could have taken the job away from me. Not even Shack.

Have I blown that chance? Maybe not. Ron's arm was so sore today during our light workout that he couldn't even throw. If I don't tell Coach Knox anything about these headaches . . .

October 21

YESTERDAY I HAD TO TELL GARY TUTHILL, OUR TRAINER, that I still had a slight headache and I wasn't sharp. Handling the quarterbacking was harder than it should have been: I had to think too much about which way I should turn after the snap, or where my receiver should be. That's not normal and frankly I was frightened. I have a good mind. I'd like to keep it.

Naturally, Tut told Coach Knox and Coach Knox told Dr. Kerlan and Dr. Kerlan called me and said he'd made an appointment with one of the best neurologists in the country, Dr. Richard Walker in the Reed Neurological Research Center at UCLA. I spent most of the day there and had to miss practice. This is our big offensive day, the most important day of the week. Now, Ron is sure to start at New Orleans.

Dr. Walker turned out to be a diminutive, soft-spoken professional who seemed to take extra time to tell me what was happening to me. First he gave me an electroencephalogram —called an EEG for short—to see what was happening to my brain. "This is going to hurt a bit," the doctor said, then proceeded to stick about twenty-five needles in my head. They hurt all right—every time I moved. The needles were connected to a machine that measured my brain waves— which showed up on a calibrated chart as a series of peaks and valleys.

Then the doctor put me in a darkened room—on a bed— and I fell asleep. About an hour later the doctor came back, woke me up, read the chart, asked me a few questions and explained that my fuzziness would go away in a day or two.

"You've got to expect this," he said, "after a slight concussion." And to make sure I understood, he spent about twenty minutes explaining what happens to a person's mental processes in a concussion.

His analysis came as something of a relief. My first fear revolved around my ability to think—a pretty basic thing and something that I'd like to go on doing for the foreseeable future. My second fear, that I wouldn't be able to play anymore, was a lesser worry. I know that football isn't—and won't be—the only thing in my life. But right now it is way ahead of whatever is in second place. I enjoy the game more than I had realized. And now I know that I can play it with the best of them. I hope I get another chance to prove that.

We leave for New Orleans after a light workout tomorrow. Sin City. Bourbon Street. Girlie joints. Bob Klein says the Rams always have trouble winning in New Orleans. Too many distractions. Some of the guys like to cut loose there.

Tom Dempsey, who is a disc jockey in bayou country during the off-season, says he is going to fix me up with a Cajun girl. Sure. I need that like I need—twenty-five needles in my head.

October 22

WE HAD A LIGHT LUNCH ON THE PLANE, THEN SETTLED down to watch Neil Simon's *Murder By Death* on the in-flight movie. What I saw of it was good. Rich Saul kept switching my channel on me and blowing in my earphone. Rich is a great big hulking lineman from Michigan State. On the field, one of the best centers in the league. Off the field, he is a teddy bear, one of the nicest guys I've ever met in my life. He has a career going in real estate in Orange County and his wife, Eileen, has gone into business with Jack Young-blood's wife, Diane. It's a quality printing business—wedding announcements and the like—located in one of the flossiest shopping centers around, Orange Coast Plaza, and business couldn't be better. Because these gals are wives of the two Rams stars, they got a big writeup in the L.A. *Times,* Orange County edition. After that, business boomed. They can hardly handle it all. Another one of the Rams' hidden fringe benefits.

We are staying at the Marriott Hotel. Carl Ekern, my roommate, and I have a room overlooking the wide, muddy Mississippi. One of the things I don't like about our travels is this: we're so occupied with game preparations that we have very little time to get out and see the towns we're in. We come in on a bus, go straight to the hotel, just have time for drinks and dinner and have to be back for our bed check. Tomorrow we're in team meetings and a workout until three o'clock. We have six hours to see the town and have to be back in the hotel for another meeting at nine, followed by a hamburger buffet and bed check at eleven. Unless you have friends who want to show you the town, you're in a vacuum.

I am lucky in New Orleans, however. I have a friend here, Walter Isaacson, a native of New Orleans, Harvard grad and a guy who just finished two years as a Rhodes scholar. He is now a reporter for the *Times-Picayune* and he will show me around a bit tomorrow.

Tonight we saw Bourbon Street on our own. It was a short walk from our hotel and Rob Scribner, Bob Klein and I hit the street shortly after we arrived. The Rams have us all pre-registered, so getting in is no hassle.

Bourbon Street was both less and more than I expected. I wanted to see more places with live music. Instead, I saw far more than I wanted of barkers, dirty gutters, hookers, garish signs advertising peep shows, nude dancers—and tourists, like ourselves. Scrib and Bob and I stopped in front of one bar where a he-she tried to entice us inside. "Let's go in," said Scrib.

"What is it?" I said.

Scrib just raised his eyebrows.

"It's a transsexual bar," said Klein.

We passed on the transsexuals, found a place called Felix's that was supposed to have good oysters and talked about the Rams and the season. "We're a lot better than we've showed so far," said Klein.

"The defense has done well," said Scrib. We agreed on that. Our front four were staying healthy. Jack Youngblood and Fred Dryer were at their prime. Larry Brooks, in his fifth year, was just reaching his. Merlin Olsen, in his fifteenth year, was still playing All-Pro ball. The four of them weren't getting as many sacks as last year, but they were tougher on everybody's running attack. And this year they didn't have to try for as many sacks—because we had a better secondary. Monte Jackson was leading the league in interceptions and Rod Perry was right behind him. These two sophomore cornerbacks were becoming the best in the league. Which is to say they were two of the best athletes in the league. A cornerback has to run backward as fast as a wide receiver can run forward. He has to be smart and quick and learn about forty-five different defensive formations every week. And for second-year men, both Jackson and Perry had extraordinary savvy.

How did the Rams manage to get them both? Under the general direction of our chief talent scout, Norm Pollom, the Rams spent a lot of time and money looking for these two and gambling just a bit after they found them. Rod Perry is small, only five nine and 170; and he had undergone surgery on his knee after his junior year at Colorado. But, hoping, the Rams drafted him way up in the fourth round in 1975. Monte Jackson didn't come from Ohio State, a school that produces some of the finest defensive backs in the country, he played at San Diego State, but Pollom insisted the Rams go for him early in the 1975 draft because he'd seen Monte Jackson do some incredible things in a very pass-conscious league. Both gambles seem to have paid off and are likely to pay dividends for years to come.

Our veteran safety men, Dave Elmendorf of Texas, and Bill Simpson of Michigan State, have provided the two younger men with the kind of steadying influence they needed. Coverage by the four of them, under the careful tutelage of Jim Wagstaff, gets better and better each week.

So does our linebacker play. Jim Youngblood, in his fourth year, out of Tennessee Tech, subbing for Rick Kay, keeps improving at left linebacker. Butch Robertson, on the other side, doesn't have to. Jack Reynolds, at middle linebacker, keeps them all working together. And Jack (we call him Hack) is a real student of the game. At team meetings he writes down everything that is said—and always carries at least a dozen well-sharpened pencils with him at all times so he'll never be caught short. That's a little compulsive and a little crazy, too, but then linebackers have to be a little crazy. When Reynolds played at Tennessee he was even more intense, I am told, than he is now. Once after his Volunteers lost a tough game, he was so angry he went home and sawed an old '55 Chevy in half, right down the middle with a hacksaw. (That's why we call him Hack.) It took him a day and a half, he says, and after that he felt better.

But Hack's buddy, Butch Robertson, is the freest spirit on the team. Crazy, too. Butch is a lover of life, he revels in it. He has a booming T-shirt business (a nice adjunct to a salary that must be in excess of $75,000) and among his shirts is a blue and gold number that reads "RAMS." "You gotta have permission from the league for that, don't you?" says Jerry Wilcox, one of our two p.r. men, on the bus today.

"What do you mean?" says Butch, his eyes twinkling.

"NFL Properties put all these things out on a franchise basis: banners, pennants, sweat shirts, T-shirts, everything. That way, the league and the team get a royalty on all sales."

"Not on my T-shirts, they don't," says Butch. "I looked around and I found a high school that uses the name 'Rams.' The Huntington Beach Rams. And their colors are blue and gold. So I made a deal with the high school. I've got *their* permission to make Rams T-shirts. And I don't pay them any royalty at all." He pulls a cigarette out of his leather purse with an air of insouciance and sticks it between his teeth, right in the middle of his mouth. "Got a light, Jerry?" He smiles, pleased with himself. With his new drooping moustache, he looks to me like nothing so much as a pirate.

But Butch is not a pirate. In fact, he has contributed much of his time for each of the past several summers coaching Little League baseball in Huntington Beach. He takes cast-offs, kids nobody else wants to draft, and works with them by the hour, making them into pretty fair imitations of real ball players. And each year Butch's transformed castoffs win their league championship. His alumni have formed a group, Robertson's Raiders. They come to Rams games now, en masse, and cheer for Butch—and the Rams. Not that Butch needs his own cheering section. I have never met a man with more self-confidence. Or a man who wanted more to win. Each game he dedicates to someone near and dear to him. The New Orleans game, he says, will be for his mother and father. Naturally, to Butch, they are the smartest parents God ever made.

Butch was christened Isiah when he was born here in New Orleans and was a star athlete at Pine View High in Covington, Louisiana. From there he went to Southern University, a black school in Baton Rouge that never gets much ink in the sporting press. Nevertheless, he was named an All-American by *The Sporting News* and by *Time* and a Small College All-American by AP and UPI. Lots of raw talent there. His first year with the Rams, he was named Defensive Rookie of the Year by the AP, a shooting star. But Butch's brilliance didn't help the Rams that much: they were eight, five and one on the season and it was obvious to the veterans like Merlin Olsen that Butch was going to have to learn to play with the team rather than on his own. He did learn and now he is one of the canniest linebackers in the business. Just ask him!

Sitting there in Felix's, eating oysters and drinking beer, Scrib and Klein and I also agreed that something was wrong with our offense. We had the personnel. But we weren't playing our best. Why? Probably the quarterback situation. Good offensive play implies a lot of teamwork—the metaphor of a well-oiled machine is not a bad one. But, because our quarterbacks kept getting injured, we kept putting a new, unoiled part in the machine each week. And a damned important part at that.

"It'd be better if one quarterback would get in there and stay there," said Klein. Scrib agreed. Neither of them tried to spare my feelings. Both said Shack ought to be the one. I had to agree. I didn't want to. But, hell, I hadn't proved enough—yet. I was only a rookie. I had to defer to the universal opinion of my elders: Shack ought to be the one.

Even if he turns out to be *the* quarterback, Klein and Scrib feel the team still has problems. I am not sure whether they really believe this or not or just repeat what they read in the papers; but they said they thought the coaches were holding back the offense. "We're not loose enough," said Klein. "Too conservative. I don't like to see us nursing a four-point lead. We get ahead by four points and then settle down to three plunges and a punt, waiting for the other team to make mistakes."

Klein amended his criticism to a degree: it was worse last year. This year there's been a real attempt to put more unpredictability in the offense.

Still and all, Coach Knox is a man who plays percentage ball. He'd rather have the sure three points on an easy field goal than take a chance on making a first down on the 15, even if it's early in the game.

October 23

WALTER ISAACSON, MY RHODES SCHOLAR FRIEND WITH THE soft accents of the bayou, picked me up today and took me around town. He showed me the shoals where a big riverboat had gone aground a couple of days ago and dozens of lives were lost. At the Superdome, which was supposed to cost $80 million and ended up costing $200 million, he told me, "A lot of politicians got fat on this project." Walter specializes in political reporting at the *Times-Picayune*. And he introduced me to some more great oyster bars. I wish I could meet interesting reporters like Walter in every town I visit. I don't like coming into a town, playing a game and then leaving it in a rush without knowing any more about it than I did before.

When I got back to the Marriott, Shack and Harold Jackson were there in the lobby with their families. I enjoyed meeting each of them. Nice people. Shack's mother really looks young. I told Harold's mother what a great receiver he is. "Harold's going to make *me* famous," I said.

October 24

As predicted, the Saints weren't easy. For three quarters, we stuttered, stumbled and fumbled along. Ron Jaworski was sacked three times for a loss of 29 yards and he had only gained 15 yards on three out of eleven completions, which gave him a net of minus 14. And two interceptions.

We had a lead of 10–0 at the half, but our only touchdown came after a critical New Orleans fumble on their own 19, where Larry Brooks jarred the ball loose from Chuck Muncie, the fine rookie from Cal. Merlin Olsen recovered at the 15 and it was McCutcheon, Cappelletti, McCutcheon on three plays for the TD.

After the intermission we were still stuttering, but the Saints started marching in. Saints Coach Hank Stram substituted Bobby Douglass for Bobby Scott and Douglass passed in the second half alone for 285 yards. At the end of the third quarter the score read L.A. 10–New Orleans 7.

"Warm up, Pat," Coach Knox told me.

The Saints had the ball on our 13 and were driving. With fourth down and two to go on our 5, Stram settled for the points to tie and Rick Szaro kicked the field goal.

I took the helm with 13:14 to go on our own 29. There in the huddle everyone seemed a foot taller than I. Milking the humor in the situation, Tom Mack told me to stand up. "I *am* standing up," I said.

"Oh," said Mack, laughing. Everyone was laughing. I liked that. And laughing together we quickly drove to our 43. Then Rod Phillips, in for Cappelletti, who had pulled a muscle, fumbled. Damn. And Rod was normally so sure-handed, too. This wasn't our day.

We stopped the Saints again, Tom Blanchard punted for the eighth time on this day and we tried again from our 25. On first down I overthrew Harold Jackson. Double damn. He was clear, too. On two running plays Phillips picked up 16 yards, then was held for no gain, and we were penalized back to the 31 for holding. On second and fifteen I faded to pass, found no one and tried to run up the middle. A 5-yard sack. Triple damn. On third and twenty Stram put in his nickel defense, that defense swarmed the receivers and my pass to Jessie was knocked down. Quadruple damn. I wasn't doing any better than Ron was. We just weren't jelling. But I had to hang in there.

Thank God, again, for our defense. They gave up two yards to Chuck Muncie, Youngblood sacked Douglass for a 14-yard loss and Hacksaw Reynolds became Hawkshaw Reynolds when he sniffed a draw to Tony Galbreath and threw him for a 2-yard loss. Cullen Bryant returned Blanchard's 31-yard punt to the Saints' 40 and Kenny Myer sent me in with a play action pass, 29 FX Post.

We'd worked on this play all week. It was designed to capitalize on the aggressiveness of their free safety, Tommy Myers of Syracuse. The play called for Ron Jessie to cut over the middle, I'd fake to him and hope that Myers would come up on him while Harold Jackson looped behind him in the end zone.

"Three-thirty eight!" I shouted over the ball, calling out numbers that meant absolutely nothing, a fake audible. "Three-thirty eight—Hike. Hike!" I dropped back quickly, looking over my left shoulder at Jessie. He started his cut over the middle, but I didn't have enough time. Their right tackle was right on top of me, so I stepped forward into the pocket. That did it. That move gave me time to fake to Jessie, Myers came up on him and I zipped the ball down the middle to Harold.

There were 60,000 people in that stadium, but I didn't hear a sound. As I got up off the ground (I don't know who hit me as I threw), I guessed that I had thrown the ball through the end zone. But no. The ref had his arms raised, signaling a touchdown. But it was weird. Usually there's some kind of noise after a TD, if only the groans of the home fans. Here: nothing. I ran down the field, shook Harold's hand, then ran back to the bench. In almost total silence. It was like a dream.

Dempsey missed the extra point, our defense held the Saints, and again we had the ball: 5:50 left. Could we eat up all that time? No. After a couple of running losses we ended up with third and seventeen. Clutch ran for 10 yards to our 25, but we got yet another holding penalty on the play and the New Orleans fans started to go crazy again.

A dilemma for Hank Stram: should he give us a chance to punt with fourth and seven on our 25? Or take the penalty and give us another chance with third and twenty-four on our 8-yard line? He preferred to put the rookie under pressure and took the penalty.

I liked that. I sent Jessie streaking down the right sideline. He was covered pretty well, but I had confidence in him. Standing close to my own goal, I put the ball up. It went almost 50 yards in the air and I thought I had overthrown it. But Jessie got under it and we had a first down on our 45. That gave us the breathing space we needed. I would have preferred a sustained drive here, running *and* passing. Stram was ready for what we did do instead: three straight plunges into the line got us only 9 yards. We punted.

But Rusty Jackson got off a good one, fair caught on the Saints' eleven. They had 89 yards to go for a TD. Bobby Douglass gave getting there a noble try. On eleven straight pass plays he moved the Saints down to our 26—where Tony Galbreath fumbled after a tackle by Jim Youngblood—four seconds on the clock, Rams 16–Saints 10.

In the dressing room Coach Knox was subdued. We hadn't played well. He wasn't happy. But he'd take the win. He came over to me and said quietly, "Good game." Then he went over to Ron Jaworski, several lockers to my left. "It wasn't your fault, Ron. We weren't blocking very well today." Ron was almost purple with frustration, his head down between his knees.

I turned to Shack. "Ron O.K.?" I said.

"He's all right," Shack said.

We were both concerned about Ron. What happened out there today *wasn't* his fault. I'd gotten sacked, too, twice, and I'd thrown some bad balls as well. But I was lucky. I threw two bombs that were caught and that made all the difference in this game. I was a hero and Ron was a goat.

I knew I had to be careful what I said to the reporters, who were all over me, blind to Ron. "I was just lucky," I said. "I've thrown better passes. Harold made a good catch. Ron could have done the same things I did if he had been in there in the fourth quarter. Things just seemed to break right for me. Really, I was just lucky."

Carroll Rosenbloom came up to me. "Good job, Pat."

Doug Krikorian of the *Herald-Examiner* wanted to know whether I was now going to stake a claim on the job of number one quarterback. "No," I said. "The job is Shack's. He'll be ready next week." Anyway, that's what most of my teammates believed. I'd lose everything I'd gained this season by "staking a claim" in the press to Shack's job. If the coaches wanted to change that, well, that was up to them.

On the flight home Rich Saul, our great center, was trying to piece out the puzzle. Why did the line, his offensive line, have so much trouble today? "I think," he said, "they were reading our wig-wag signals from the sideline. You notice that your two big plays, the long passes? They weren't called by wig-wag. You talked to Kenny at the sideline, then you came in and called the plays. I think they have cracked our code."

I doubted that they had. But it was possible. They seemed to be teeing off on the quarterback on almost every pass play. Maybe they *did* know. . . . I got a play-by-play from Jerry Wilcox and studied it. Maybe, just maybe. . . . In the second quarter, with the Rams ahead 10–0, with two minutes remaining, at a time when we'd be likely to keep the ball on the ground, McCutcheon lost a yard, then Jaworski got sacked twice in a row trying to pass. We punted, and then when we got the ball back again, Ron threw incomplete to Jessie *on first down* (when there was no semaphore: Ron had brought the play in from the bench) under no particular rush. But then, on wig-wagged plays, Ron was hit as he threw hurriedly to McCutcheon and was sacked again by Derland Moore. As Arte Johnson used to say on "Laugh-In," "Very interesting . . ."

Later, Kenny Myer came by. "You seem to have the luck, kid."

Most of the team had started watching *Bingo Long and the Traveling All-Stars* on the in-flight movie. I was trying to read *Burr* by Gore Vidal. Nobody was watching me, so I allowed myself to smile. "Yep," I said to Kenny. "Yep." I had made a believer out of Kenny Myer.

The team plane got home early, about 9 P.M. and Butch Robertson, hurt but not badly, late in the game, had a girl-friend waiting in a big black limousine to comfort him in his pain. I drove home in my Pinto but I was still too keyed up to call it a night. Cindy and I went over to a bar on Third Street called Chuck's, near our apartment. The bartender did a double-take when we sat down. "You look like Pat Haden," he said, "but Pat Haden's in New Orleans. I saw him on the tube."

I laughed and said that Patty's back in town. "Well, now," he said, as if it were a great honor for him to serve Pat and Cindy Haden. He bought us a couple of rounds. A waiter whom I had known at SC came over. Others in the bar crowded around.

October 25

THE CRITICS' CORNER: I GOT A TENTATIVE ENDORSEMENT from Professor Oates in the *Times* and Ron Jaworski got some ridicule he didn't deserve from Doug Krikorian in the *Examiner*.

> In the fourth quarter [wrote Oates] the Rams did do one thing right. They got Haden in there. This was the second time the USC rookie has delivered the winning pass for this team—though he hasn't played that much—and in his two starts this year held Fran Tarkenton to 10–10 and led Chicago 10–0, until knocked out by injury. Maybe Haden isn't the whole answer, and maybe he isn't even the answer—it's too early to tell—but he does seem to make things happen.

> Jaworski eliminated himself yesterday [wrote Krikorian] under the magnificent Louisiana Superdome with a performance so insufferably inadequate that Knox mercifully removed him after three quarters. Jaworski once predicted he would become another Sammy Baugh, but you now figure he was mistaken. Why, he has a better chance of becoming Sammy Davis.

But Mal Florence of the *Times* had a more analytical piece that raised interesting questions about our troubled offensive line. He noted we have had ten holding penalties in the last three games. (We actually had two more than we got "credit" for, because Coach Stram had his troops refuse holding penalties twice last Sunday in New Orleans.)

After an interview with Coach Ray Prochaska, offensive line coach, and Tom Mack, our eleven-year veteran guard, Florence concluded that game officials were not only getting pickier on their penalty calls, they were being inconsistent as well. Mack said, "I've been called for holding four times this season and two were good calls and two were bad. The bad ones came on running plays and, over the years, they don't call much holding on running plays."

Another problem is the change in blocking rules four years ago that made it O.K. for an offensive lineman to extend his arms and hit a defensive player on the chest—as long as his elbows weren't locked and he didn't extend his arms past the rusher's shoulder pads. But say Tom Mack hits a rusher in the chest and the rusher turns sideways. Then one of Mack's hands is on his back. The official sees that happen and throws a flag for holding. "That," said Mack, "is how you can get into trouble with this newer technique."

Why did the league make the rule change at all? Because defensemen were getting stronger and stronger. The only way they could think of to equalize the fight in the pits was to give the blockers a little more help. I'm for that, 110 percent. If my pass blockers don't block, I can't pass. I can also get maimed under the charge of four linemen who probably total out at about a half ton. Or picked up by a 230-pound linebacker who lifts weights the year around and tossed into the fifth row.

October 26

DAY OFF TODAY. YESTERDAY, IN OUR LIGHT WORKOUT, I took the practice—while Ron Jaworski and James Harris stood to the side and watched me do it. Kenny Myer told me to. I wonder: are they thinking of starting me this Sunday against Seattle? I heard that at his weekly breakfast with the press this morning, Coach Knox gave some hints that I would. He said, "Right now, Pat Haden is our only healthy quarterback. Jaworski is still not a hundred percent . . . Pat played very well this week. He makes things happen . . . He has the ability to give us the big play. He's been a winner throughout his career."

Tonight the Rams had me go out to the Montclair Shopping Center near Ontario, to the May Company, and sign autographs. There was a line there about four hundred yards long and they had me signing my name for two hours. Mom and Dad came by toward the end and watched me for a while, then I went back to the house with them and had a glass of wine. They do not get out often enough, so I told them I was reserving the Tower Room at the Bel Air Hotel for them on the night of November 20. That's a Saturday night, the eve of the SC-UCLA game. The Rams will be in San Francisco for a big one against the 49ers, who are still ahead of us in the division standings.

October 27

TODAY, AT BREAKFAST, SHACK WOULDN'T LOOK AT ME.
There is some tension between us now, because the papers
have been full of speculation this week over who's going to
start at quarterback. A reporter for *Pro Football West* asked
an old Ram hero, Bob Waterfield, what he thought about the
Rams quarterbacks. He said he thought Harris is "slow to
get the ball away and has trouble finding a secondary receiver.
They say he can throw the long ball, but he really has to
wind up to do it." Jaworski? "He lacks a little touch on short
passes, can't seem to take anything off. However, the potential
is there." Which Rams quarterback has the most potential?
Said Waterfield: "Pat Haden." I do not know if Shack has
read this or some of the other stuff that has appeared this
week, but now he has nervous eyes.

But Knox hasn't said who'll start. All three of us have to
prepare. And, Coach Knox says, one of us, or all of us are
going to have to score more. Our defense is on the field too
much, we've had too many penalties, too many turnovers.
We've fumbled four or five times when we had the ball inside
our opponent's 5-yard line. That's throwing away points. New
England and Baltimore and Oakland don't do that. They
score. We're going to have to develop a killer instinct. We
have to bury somebody. Why not Seattle? That may sound
easy. Seattle has beaten only Tampa Bay. But they had Dallas
down 14–0 and Green Bay 20–0, they gave St. Louis a good
game, 24–30. And in the preseason, the game I started, we
only beat them 16–13.

We think we can win best by keeping the ball away from

them. That means keeping the ball ourselves. We may be able to throw against both of their cornerbacks, deep on Eddie McMillan, a former Ram, who plays too tight, and under Rolly Woolsey, who plays off a lot.

October 28

SHACK TOOK OVER TODAY IN PRACTICE. KNOX STILL HASN'T said who's starting Sunday, but this move toward Shack has helped ease the tension between him and me. This is good because we have more important things to think about. Too many things, says Shack. The coaches have us working on a lot more audibles than usual this week. If the linebackers back off a yard, that's one audible. If the same linebackers get down in a three-point stance, that's another audible. If they step off a bit, that's yet another. "This might be the wrong week for all these audibles," Shack says. "Seattle's not that good and we oughta just blow 'em out of the Coliseum."

I tend to agree; coming up to the ball in practice this week, I find that I have too much to think about. If I miss the particular defensive "look," and don't call the audible, the coaches will get mad. If I haven't called an audible and I am into my count I will be wondering whether I should have called one. It hurts my concentration a little bit.

Maybe we're all thinking a little too much. I have good natural ability. I like to let my good instincts take over. Read the coverage? Hell, I saw Tarkenton the other day on film. On this particular play he didn't read the coverage as he faded to pass. He just turned his back to the play, hauled back deep and quick and looked for the open man.

Tonight, despite my reservations about celebrities-in-politics, I was guest of honor at a dinner-dance to raise funds for Lou Brutocao, the Mayor of West Covina, who is running for Congress. I played football with Lou's son Rudy, who was student body president and a liberal, then, and I finally told Rudy I'd do it. His dad's a Republican and I'm a Democrat, but I know his dad. As I told the group at dinner, "Lou's a good, honest, strong, moral, decent, hard-working guy. You won't find him on the golf course when he should be studying some new legislation. And you won't find him paying your tax dollars to secretaries who can't type."

Rudy's the same kind of guy. He's not a professional politico. He's in med school at UCLA and will finish this June. Rudy says the people aren't well served by any Congressman who's in office too long—and his dad will sponsor a bill when and if he gets to Congress that will limit a Congressman to four terms.

I have been trying to watch the progress of this Presidential campaign, listen to the debates and talk things over with guys on the team like Tom Mack. Right now I am not too sure whom I will vote for. I am disappointed when I realize that both candidates have avoided talking much about a major policy question that will affect the future of us all: how much of our national substance are we spending on the military— and how much should we be spending? I am undecided. Eighty percent of the time I think we are foolish to appropriate the billions we spend on "defense" when at the same time our cities (and many of the people in them) are falling apart. But I do not have all the facts. I would like to see a full-scale national debate on this question. Advocates for the military-industrial complex keep telling us that we're falling behind in the arms race. But when we ask for facts and figures, we have to take their numbers on faith—and from people whose testimony is tainted by their own self-interest.

Or, they give us no numbers at all; they say they are "classified." This bothers me. I think the people have a right to know. And our elected representatives have a duty to find out. I lean to Carter because he seems more concerned about this issue and some other people-oriented issues than President Ford. But Ford's a decent guy and is catching up to Carter in the polls. Carter had such a big lead. If he loses now, it will be the biggest throwaway in the history of American politics.

This week in L.A. I've seen César Chavez's farmworkers all over town. They're carrying huge placards urging a "Yes" vote on Proposition 14. It's an initiative that would force growers to allow secret-ballot elections, something that has already been put into law by the Legislature in Sacramento but has been derailed by a coalition of Republicans and rural Democrats controlling the appropriations.

I hope Proposition 14 passes. If this means that the price of grapes or green beans goes up a few cents, I am willing to pay it. And so should anyone who is interested in bread and justice for these poor farmworkers. Since 1936 most American workers can decide by secret ballot whether or not they want a union. Pressures from the farm bloc excepted farmworkers. That's not fair.

October 30

WE PLAY SEATTLE TOMORROW IN THE COLISEUM, BUT ONLY last night did we learn that Shack will be starting QB. I agree with that decision. After all, Shack is nineteen and five with the Rams. He's got the track record. But we all wish Coach Knox would make up his mind sooner. It bothers us, not knowing. Before the Chicago game he didn't tell us until Friday. Before New Orleans it was Thursday.

Ron, naturally, is down. He hears Knox tell him the foulups at New Orleans weren't his fault, but as Knox is telling him this, he is yanking him. For what? "I don't know how I could go from the penthouse to the outhouse in one week," Ron says.

October 31

JACK YOUNGBLOOD WAS STANDING IN THE COLISEUM DRESSing room after the game with one towel wrapped around his middle and another around his neck, talking to the press. I stopped a moment to listen, because I liked what I heard him saying. "What happened today is that we came to realize we had matured enough to stop screwing around and barely winning games against teams we should beat easily. To be a great team like the old Baltimore Colts or Miami, you have to be able to immediately capitalize on opponents' mistakes and knock 'em out. The way we've been playing the last couple of weeks, one wrong bounce of the ball and we could have been a game and a half behind the Forty-Niners. But today we jumped on 'em."

We sure as hell did: 24–0 at the end of the first quarter. We scored every time we got the ball. And Monte Jackson picked off a swing pass by Seattle's great scrambler Jim Zorn and returned it 41 yards for a touchdown. After six carries McCutcheon hurt his knee. Coach Knox said, "We're going to give you a rest today, Clutch," and put in Jim Bertelsen. No difference. We kept scoring.

In all, Shack completed fourteen out of twenty-five passes

105

for 208 yards and two touchdowns. Harold Jackson caught five of them for 86 yards. Rod Phillips ran impressively. He got 86 yards in twelve carries for a 7.17 average, our best ball carrier of the day. Except for me: I averaged 12 yards a carry today (on one carry). Coach Knox put me in with a few minutes to go in the game and we were both pleased with that. I moved the team from midfield to the Seahawk 23 and from there, on third and sixteen, with the Seahawks playing pass, I fired a strike in the end zone to substitute receiver Tom Geredine, who has taken over for Freeman Johns, out for the year with an injured knee.

Final score: Rams 45–Seahawks 6.

Before our game was ended, good news flashed on the peristyle scoreboard. St. Louis had just beaten San Francisco 23–20. It looked like we were ahead of the 49ers at last, and we felt good about that. We got the ball back at midfield with a little over a minute to play. "O.K., Coach," I said, deadpan, to Knox before I went out to the huddle. "How about the quarterback jump pass?"

He frowned and spoke sharply. "Huh?" Then he realized I was shining him on. "Oh." He smiled and told me to go out there and send Cullen Bryant into the middle until time ran out. Which I did. But, shoot, leading 45–6, we had nothing to lose by calling an entertaining play. When all is said and done, we're in show business. We—and our loyal fans—ought to have a little more fun. This isn't Armageddon. It's a game. I think.

To everyone, that is, except Ron Jaworski. He was the only one who didn't play today. Afterward he dressed without showering and left the locker room angry.

November 2

ELECTION DAY. IT LOOKS LIKE JIMMY CARTER HAS WON. BUT not by much. And that he won't carry California. The pundits say his coming out strong for the farmworkers didn't help him any here and I think they are right. Proposition 14 went down to defeat by a two-to-one margin. Those who voted against 14 probably didn't vote for Carter. I think it's as simple as that.

As for my own personal candidate, Lou Brutocao lost in his bid for Congress out in the San Gabriel Valley. Too bad. He is a good man. Maybe next time . . .

November 6

IT WAS 86 DEGREES WHEN WE LEFT L.A. THIS AFTERNOON and 43 degrees when we landed in Latonia, Kentucky, a twenty-minute bus ride across the Ohio River to Cincinnati. On the plane we watched Mel Brooks' *Silent Movie,* had a snack and were ready for dinner as soon as we checked into Stouffer's Inn, downtown. A television crew filmed us as we picked up our keys and somebody asked a cameraman if they shot all the teams that came into town or was it just the Rams. "All of them," he said. "This is big news in a small town." Cincinnati may be "small town" but it is in the heart of big football country and they are expecting a capacity crowd for the game, even though it is on "Monday Night Football."

Rusty Jackson, who says he's superstitious, got room 1313 and he's expecting the worst. I hope that doesn't mean he will have any of his punts blocked Monday night. Our last appearance witnessed by Howard, Alex and Frank didn't help our national reputation very much. It was the 0–16 beating we took from the 49ers.

Our week has been a dull one. Just the way Chuck Knox likes it: no Quarterback Controversy. Just a good, workmanlike preparation *by* a good football team *for* a good football team. Bill Johnson, the Bengals' head coach, is helping Cincinnati fans reconcile themselves to the loss of Paul Brown on the sidelines. They have only lost two games, 27–28 to the potent Baltimore Colts and 6–23 to the sleeping giants, the Pittsburgh Steelers, who had lost four of their first five when the Bengals came to Pittsburgh.

The next three weeks will make or break our season. We play three playoff contenders, Cincinnati, St. Louis, San Francisco. We can beat all of them. Question is: will we? We can't fool around against any of them. They'll capitalize on anything we give them.

November 7

WE WORKED OUT FOR AN HOUR OR SO THIS MORNING AT Riverfront Stadium, in our blue knit caps and gray sweat suits—all of us except Tackle Doug France, who was wearing only a pair of shorts and a T-shirt on this near-freezing day. Doug will have a lot of friends watching him here from his alma mater, Ohio State, and he will have his job cut out for him. He'll be matched against Coy Bacon, a former Ram,

108

General Manager Don Klosterman (left), Carroll Rosenbloom, owner of the Rams, and Vice President Steve Rosenbloom. They run the business.

(VIC STEIN)

Head Coach Charles Robert Knox. No American Army general ever made more intensive preparations for a battle.

(PETER READ MILLER)

Our offensive coordinator Kenny Myer sent in almost all of our plays with an elaborate sideline semaphore.

(GEORGE LONG)

Defensive coordinator Ray Malavesi called all of our coverages. Here, he sends in a change with Free Safety Bill Simpson.

(GEORGE LONG)

After we beat Atlanta 59–0 at home, the biggest margin of victory in Rams history, CBS's Paul Hornung interviewed Merlin Olsen. It was Ole's last game in the Coliseum, after 15 All-Pro seasons.

(JON WALDNER)

In our last regular game of the season, against Detroit, my cleats caught in the Astroturf. I twisted my knee and thought I was finished for the season, if not for life. Trainer Garrett Giemont on my right, equipment aide Todd Hewitt on my left.

(GEORGE GELLATLY)

But I was wrong. The very next week, in the playoffs, our supposedly gimpy quarterback crossed up Dallas and ran 7 yards for a TD. We won 14–12.

(WIDE WORLD PHOTOS)

In the locker-room exultation after the Dallas victory, offensive linemen John Williams, Doug France and Dennis Harrah led our chant for our "Dee-fense!"

(WIDE WORLD PHOTOS)

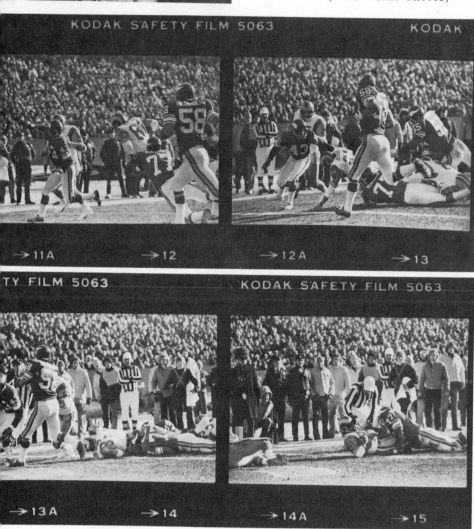

Here's Ron Jessie's near-TD in the championship game at Minnesota. In frame 12, Mark Mullaney has hold of Jessie. In frame 13, Jessie is going down. In frame 14, he's down and the ball is clearly across the goal. You be the judge.

(JAMES ROARK)

who has been quoted a lot lately about his vendetta against L.A. The playing surface is awful. Solid concrete with a thin rug on top; I think they call it Astroturf and I hate it. Larry Brooks came running out, did a rolling tumble on the 20-yard line and said, "God! Nobody fall on this stuff." But of course we'll be playing football here, not baseball, and two forty-three-man squads will be falling here for three hours Monday night. It doesn't make much sense to me. Both clubs have millions of dollars invested in their talent—and they put that talent to work under conditions that are nothing but dangerous.

Jonathan Winters is with the team on this trip. He's a never-miss-a-game Rams fan and the Rams enjoy having him come along on at least one road game a year; he has family in the area here, so this one seemed like a good idea. On the flight he sat in front of the plane and entertained some of the coaches and the press. Today he dropped by my room to talk a while with me and Carl Ekern.

Winters has a fine mind—although, he told us, it is one that gets him into trouble from time to time. I'll say this: you have to be on the alert with him. One moment he'll be Johnny Winters asking some serious questions about our game plan and then, without warning, he'll slip into a "bit." It is up to his listeners to guess whom he's "doing." One time it will be one of his stock characters, like Maude Frickert. Another time he will just ease into a new role he is trying on for size: our United Airlines captain, one of the stewardesses, an anonymous member of the Bengals' defensive line.

Is Winters always on stage? I was told that last night, at dinner with two of my writer friends who are here, he revealed more and more of himself as the evening wore on— and ended up at two A.M. talking seriously with one of them about the lifelong anguish he has had dealing with his own father. There a different, serious Jonathan Winters emerged.

117

He says he is working on his own autobiography. That is one I'd like to read.

We watched some of the pro games on TV today, a rare treat, since most Sundays we are playing and can't watch. The Cardinals beat Mike Boryla and the Eagles, but not by much, 17–14. And San Francisco lost to the Redskins. That doesn't hurt us any. Tomorrow will be a long day. We are already prepared for the Bengals but we have to sit through more team meetings in the morning, then wait—a long time—for the game, which doesn't start until 9 P.M. Pat McInally just came by to say hello. He is the Bengals' punter from Harvard and an almost-Rhodes scholar whom I met at some post-season banquets in 1975. Pat is very interested in fine art and spent much of the year just touring galleries in Europe. Pat grew up in Southern California and I think Cincinnati is just a little bit dull for him. He seems bemused by the fact that the Bengals' season ticket holders do not fit any stereotypical notions of your average pro football fan. "It's a very social group," he says. "If you look around, you'll see a lot of minks and expensive leather flasks in the stands."

I'll probably have plenty of time to look around. There doesn't seem to be any hope that I'll play. And I am worried about our chances. I think we are going to play a very conservative game. Bob Klein noted that Georgia Tech beat Notre Dame yesterday without throwing a single pass. "God," I said, "I hope Coach Knox doesn't see that." But of course I'm sure he already has.

November 8

AT BREAKFAST I LEARNED THAT RUSTY JACKSON WAS PASSING blood all night. He went to the hospital this morning where the doctors diagnosed kidney stones—the result of a blow he took in the game last week—and managed to move them without surgery. The big question now is whether Rusty can bounce back enough to do our punting tonight. Right now, he's in a morphine cloud.

Also at breakfast, I found a column in today's *Enquirer* called "The Rhodes Scholar," by Tom Callahan. I'm not even scheduled to play and this guy does a whole column on me. Callahan and I talked for about fifteen minutes yesterday after our workout, but I only recognize a few of my quotes. Callahan wrote that he was disappointed when he heard I'd signed with the Rams, interpreting this move as a "sellout"— whatever that means. I had to convince him that nothing had changed in my life. "I'm going back to Oxford, January to June, the next two years," I told him. That seemed to mollify him. But I don't know why playing pro football ought to imply any kind of malefaction on my part. As a matter of fact, being a Ram in L.A. triggers so many opportunities that none of us have to "sell out" to anyone. For one thing, a man who has a good career with the Rams can earn (and save) quite a bit of money—so much that he may never have to run the risk of getting lost in a big corporation or even of working for somebody else.

With too much time on my hands today I took a short sightseeing trip in town, up to Mount Adams, a high promontory overlooking the Ohio River. I heard that Mount

119

Adams' old Victorian houses had become newly fashionable for Cincinnati's affluent, younger set and that the neighborhood was filled with quaint little shops. I found out that report was only partially true. What I did see of Mount Adams were some old houses with very interesting views of the river and the city and a few boutiques, gift shops and waterbed stores—and a few bars showing absolutely no signs of life at midday on a Monday. Maybe, I thought, there's something happening here in the evenings. But not now. . . .

I looked inside a quaint old Catholic church and thought, briefly, about what a turnoff the Church has been for me— ever since high school. I had a pastor who seemed more worried than he should have been about raising money for gold candlesticks and more marble in his church. Once he had a visiting missionary making a pitch from his pulpit for contributions to his mission. The missionary said ten dollars would feed one of his people for a month; and many of the parishioners were generous with him. Then the pastor got up in the same pulpit and asked us for more money—to buy some marble for his church—just as if he weren't even listening to the missionary's pitch. He made it clear where he was coming from. I didn't like it. And I went away sad.

I stood on a bluff and looked at the river. It looked a lot like the Mississippi, gray and muddy and, I knew, full of pollution. I remembered how the Kentuckians of Daniel Boone's time described the Ohio, blue and clear and magnificent, and this, too, made me sad. Could we ever make the industrial polluters stop pouring their offal into this once-beautiful river? We could, but I am not confident that we will. We will have to change our priorities and I am not sure that we will want to. It is too easy for the industrialists to keep the status quo by offering the people two simplistic choices: Clean rivers or jobs? I am optimistic enough to believe that there must be some tertium quid, some better way, so that we

120

can preserve nature's gifts *and* keep building a viable economy. There has to be.

In my own Los Angeles we are killing ourselves with smog. Out in the San Gabriel Valley I used to practice on days when I could hardly breathe.

Now some days (when there's a critical smog alert) the kids in school aren't even allowed to go out and play at recess. That's terrible. And why is this? Largely because the auto manufacturers have succeeded in getting delay after delay on the installation of smog controls on their cars. And the government plays along with them. A recent study by the Jet Propulsion Lab in Pasadena and Cal Tech demonstrated that the auto industry could convert to new engines that are almost totally "clean." But no one seems to be making any creative moves to do the further research and retooling necessary to make the conversion. It's easier, I guess, to keep the status quo. But that's not acceptable to me—or to many others of my generation. We put people on the moon, we can make smog-free cars. If we want to. The problem is not technological, however, it is political.

November 9

IT IS ABOUT TWO IN THE MORNING CINCINNATI TIME, OUR jet is probably somewhere over Iowa and I am angry and frustrated. We should have beaten the Bengals, but we left Riverfront Stadium losers, 20–12, and we are only a half game ahead of the 49ers.

Before 52,480 spectators, most of them Cincinnati partisans, we stuffed the ball down their throats for the entire first half. Kenny Anderson completed two passes out of twelve attempts for a total of 5 yards, the great Isaac Curtis caught zilch, and our defensive front held their two running backs, Boobie Clarke and the two-time Heisman Trophy winner, Archie Griffin, to a total of 36 yards. They didn't convert on a single third down opportunity. By contrast, we marched down the field on them time after time and got two field goals.

In the third quarter our offense fizzled and our defense was outslickered. The Bengals threw some new offensive formations or "looks" at us, put a man in motion a couple of times, forcing us into man-to-man coverage and burned us with three touchdowns.

Shack started them off by coughing up the ball on our 9-yard line and on the very next play, Anderson sent Isaac Curtis in motion to the left and ran Clark around right end. No one was there and Clark went into the end zone unmolested.

On the Bengals' next possession, Anderson scrambled for 25 yards on a third and four situation at midfield and then came right back with a pass up the middle to his tight end, Bob Trumpy, who was all alone on the goal line. Again, we were in the wrong coverage. We were in a "cover two"; they ran both wide men down the sidelines, Simpson helped out with one of them and Elmendorf with the other and Trumpy was clear right up the middle. Why was he so clear? He was Jim Youngblood's responsibility, but Jim was frozen by Anderson's fake to Clark. Trumpy went right by him. And Anderson's pass was right on the line.

Next time the Bengals got the ball they stung us again. We were running a dog, somebody dropped coverage and Boobie Clark was open for a pass in the right flat. He ran it all the way in for another score.

Naturally, our staunch defensemen were boiling after the game. Bill Simpson was telling the *Times'* Mal Florence in our somber locker room under the stadium, "Just a few missed coverages and it meant the whole damn game." He didn't come right out and blame the offense. But he came close. "Shit," he said, "we gotta get some points."

Butch Robertson was more explicit. "There's no excuse for the way our offense played. Sure, the Bengals made us make some mistakes. But that's what our offense should have been doing to them, too. If you don't have an offense that will make people make mistakes, the chances of scoring are very limited. There are too many talented people in the National Football League and you can't expect to score much with an offense as straight as ours."

I think Butch is partly right. Of course, Butch is a flamboyant personality. If he were a coach, you'd expect him to have a flamboyant offense. But too many times tonight, we'd run Cappelletti left, McCutcheon up the middle, pass incomplete and then punt. (Ailing, Rusty Jackson punted superbly, six times for a 37.7 average, almost as well as Pat McInally, who boomed one of his for 61 yards.) And the closer we got to their goal line, the more conservative we became.

With a little more than two minutes to go in the first half, we had a first down on Cincinnati's 30-yard line. It was a time to get tough, to become tigers ourselves. Instead, we were pussycats. Shack faded to throw, scrambled under a rush, retreated 14 yards and fumbled. It was only luck that our own Rich Saul recovered. But by then it was third and twenty-three on their 43. Shack overthrew Jessie and all of a sudden we were punting to them instead of driving for a TD.

I wanted to go in, in the fourth quarter. We were only behind 20–6. I felt I could have done something. In fact, we did drive deep into Bengal territory three times. The first time, Shack threw an interception on the Bengal 5. He had Ron Jessie in the clear, but the pass bounced off Ron and into the hands of Tom Casanova. The second time, we moved the ball to their 4-yard line, then Shack's handoff to Clutch was fumbled in a spot where winners cannot fumble. By the time Shack hit Jessie in the end zone for what could have been our third score of the fourth quarter there were only fifteen seconds on the clock. It was a meaningless TD. And to make it even more so, Dempsey shanked his point-after attempt.

I feel terrible. I don't feel like talking to anybody. I'm going to sleep all the way home.

November 10

WE GOT OUR SCOUTING REPORTS TODAY ON THE ST. LOUIS Cardinals. They're stronger defensively than they were last year. They've two new defensive linemen, Mike Dawson, a six four, 270-pound rookie from Arizona, at tackle, and John Zook, one of the best men in the league, obtained in a trade with Atlanta, at end. They also got Kenny Reaves from Atlanta; he's supposed to be a bad actor. And, they made a trade with the Kansas City Chiefs for Mike Sensibaugh, a really fine pass defender who played with Jack Tatum at Ohio State. Clearly, Coach Don Coryell is learning you have to have good defense to win consistently in the NFL.

The coaches all feel, however, that St. Louis is at its best when it has the ball. Jim Hart, a ten-year veteran, is one of the best quarterbacks in the game. He's got two of the league's best running backs, Jim Otis and Terry Metcalf. And a wide receiver from the Southern California Sun, Ike Harris. They'll score on us. We'll probably have to score four touchdowns to win. The way we've been scoring lately, that's going to be a big order.

November 10

CRITICS' CORNER. JIM MURPHY IN *Pro Football West:* "THE Rams scored field goals while the Bengals scored touchdowns. When that happens, touchdowns will win every time." Bob Oates in the *Times:* "In this game, the momentum changed on Harris' fumble. The worst thing Harris does is the way he handles himself when quickly or heavily rushed. He hasn't perfected the throw-away pass, he doesn't scramble quickly enough and he can't seem to hold the ball when attacked."

November 11

RON AND I WERE MISSING SHACK THIS MORNING AT BREAKfast. Then Shack came in with a funny look in his eye and slammed his play book down on the table. "Where you been?" said Jaworski. "You're late."

Shack ignored him and said to me, "You're starting this week." It was clear why he was late. He'd just come from a meeting upstairs with Coach Knox. He looked ill. I'd started before, of course, but that was when Shack was hurt. This was different. He was being benched because he had a bad game in Cincinnati.

Ron and I both felt terrible (leaving aside our own private feelings for the moment). It was unfair to him. What kind of club was this, where one bad game put you out?

"I'll tell you what kind of club it is," said Shack. "It is a club where you're only as good as your last game. You'll see. You know what's going to happen? You may think you're the local hero. But you throw a few interceptions, have a bad game or two and you'll be shipped off, too. Only I don't even know if I'll be shipped off. Maybe now nobody else will want me. That's the bad part of this whole thing."

That made me feel even worse. I was churning inside. I *was* happy to learn that I'd be starting. But I was unhappy it had to be at Shack's expense. And Ron's, too. He had a stake in this, and he was being passed over completely.

I went out and had a terrible practice today. I was throwing the ball into the dirt, sailing it out of bounds. I couldn't believe what was going on, wasn't even sure what *was* going on. Whose decision was it to bench Shack and put me in anyway? Would I ever know? Or, if I goofed up in the St. Louis game, would it even matter?

After practice I tried to sound out some of my buddies on the offensive team: Tom Mack, Ron Jessie, Larry McCutcheon. "Hey," said Clutch, "you've got nothing to do with this. Just get out there and do your best. We're not going to let it affect us."

Jessie said, "We're professionals. We do our job."

Mack said, "We've all got our pride. We're all going to play our best. Maybe, because we think it's needed now more than ever, we'll play better than our best."

That calmed me down a little. But I couldn't help thinking about what Barry Farrell had written a year ago or so in *Sport:*

Quarterbacking for the Rams [Farrell observed] is like the chairmanship of a Central American junta. The power and the glory that attach to the job are of the kind that can always be gone in the morning, and whoever he is, the maximum leader must keep himself prepared for the exile of a distant city.

November 12

I AM STILL WORRIED ABOUT JAMES HARRIS. SHACK WAS saying yesterday that "there's no room for a black quarterback in L.A." I hope he is wrong and that this was just his disappointment speaking. I do not think he was benched because he was black. In fact, some people around town are saying that if he were white he might have lost the job long ago—as John Hadl did in 1975. But the Rams hung on with Harris because they didn't want to give even the appearance of racism. Why? Because then, these same people are saying, the other blacks on the team would rebel and that'd be the end of the 1976 season.

I don't know about that. So far, I have seen no racism at all on the Rams. Hacksaw Reynolds and Butch Robertson are best friends. Shack Harris and Ron Jaworski are roommates on the road. Larry Brooks pals around with Jim Bertelsen. There is no black clique, no white clique.

But what if Shack's bitterness triggers some latent resentments among the blacks on the team? I asked Ron Jaworski about this. He's kind of bitter, too, but he doesn't think there's any racism anywhere on the Rams, not even at the top. "I just think," said Ron, "that you're starting because Carroll Rosenbloom likes you. And he doesn't like Shack."

"What do you mean?" I said. "I saw C.R. kiss Shack after the Miami game."

"Yeah, Shack was a hero at Miami, four hundred twenty-nine yards passing. If you win, C.R. loves you."

Well, yes, I thought. And what owner wouldn't? The trouble comes—on *any* team—when you *don't* win. If you aren't winning and you're black and sensitive besides, then you've got triple trouble.

But the fact is that Shack isn't getting a good press—and I am. This week everyone seemed down on Shack. John Hall did most of one column in the *Times* on the Rams' quarterback situation, reporting on a poll he had taken of some ex-Rams, including my coach at the Sun, Tom Fears. Most of them said they preferred Pat Haden. I think the number one topic around town this week is quarterbacks. KABC "Sportstalk," led by Hank Konysky, seems to draw those who are interested in nothing else. None of those who call, however, are terribly well informed. One guy phoned in today to report his own opinion: Harris, he said, isn't playing because he is seriously injured and the Rams are trying to keep it a secret. Hell, this guy is just guessing—and helping build a rumor that could hurt Shack's future. I wonder why Konysky didn't put in an immediate call to someone in the Rams organization and lay that rumor to rest. That would have been the responsible thing to do—and a piece of good reporting as well. But no, Konysky egged the caller on and said he thought there might be something to his rumor.

I know I am getting better treatment in the press than Shack is. I have one good game and I get catapulted to the top of the publicity pyramid. By what? The hopes of the fans? Probably. Hopes for what? A world-beating quarterback like Bob Waterfield? Undoubtedly. A world-beating *white* quarterback? I do not know. I am sure that some white racists in L.A. would dearly love to see the Rams led by a white quarterback. But the reverse is also true, and, for evidence of that, all I have to do, I'm told, is look in the black press.

November 13

I DON'T KNOW WHY I GET INTO THESE DINNER SPEECHES. I guess it is just that I have a hard time saying no. But I'd made a commitment long ago to a Pop Warner League at a hotel down along the Santa Ana Freeway. It has been a hard week for me, pressure really on me, phone ringing constantly at home and I really didn't want to go out and give a talk tonight, on the eve of a game I was starting, but I did. Anyway, the kids were pleased I was there. I played Pop Warner football myself, I told them. It was a good experience for me, I said our parents and our coaches insisted we play "for fun." No "winning-at-any-cost" philosophy.

Then I hit the freeway for the Beverly Hilton. Team meeting at nine o'clock, hamburger buffet at ten. No big Saturday nights for us for a while yet.

November 14

WE DIDN'T GIVE THIS GAME AWAY LIKE WE DID AT CINCINnati. We played as well as we have all season, maybe better. We made the Cards beat us in a real ding-dong battle—pro football at its best. Give the Cards credit.

I wasn't satisfied with my performance. I had opportunities that I flubbed. In the first quarter, first down on their 7-yard line, I threw an interception in the end zone. With less than a minute to go in the first half, at midfield, I threw three straight passes that went awry; we should have put some points on the board right then. But I am getting ahead of myself.

It was raining when we woke up this morning at the Beverly Hilton, drizzling when I drove downtown, still misting when we kicked off to the Cards, still cloudy during their first drive, which ended with Jim Bakken's field goal from our 23. But then a funny thing happened. As I took the field the rain stopped and the sun came out. Flourishes and trumpets for the hero of Troy. As my writer friend, Jim Murphy, put it, "all that was missing was a choir of angels singing *The Messiah.*" But I gave thanks for the sun. I needed any little break I could get. I felt that all my chips were on the table now. I'd had other chances, when Shack and Ron were hurt. This was different. Now, they were both O.K. And I was starting. I still wasn't sure why I was starting. But I knew one thing. If I didn't do well today, I'd probably be sitting on the bench for the rest of the season—and maybe a couple more seasons to come. I couldn't abide that. I'd quit first. So, in effect, my whole pro football career was on the line here and now.

All morning I was as nervous as I'd ever been in my life. Then Coach Knox had challenged us before the game: "Are you smart enough?" he asked. "Are you tough enough?" I answered to myself. Of course I was. And then my anxiety about myself faded. I was O.K.

On our first play from scrimmage, Mack, Saul and Harrah gave Clutch a good hole up the middle and he got 5 yards. On second down, they gave me all the time I needed to hit Harold Jackson on a sideline pass for 15 yards. I always like to complete my first pass of any game. It gives everyone an extra shot of confidence, in me, in themselves, in the team. And doing so early in the game was a signal to the team that Coaches Bennett, Myer and Knox had a confidence in the rookie they hadn't shown before. That helped, too. Good passing would open up our running game and give us the kind of balance Knox wanted.

"Great pass, Pat," said John Williams as we regrouped in the huddle. We moved right on down the field, mostly on the ground with McCutcheon carrying: 5 yards, 6 yards, 12 yards. Lee Bennett had me vary the attack with two passes to John Cappelletti, both identical: John ran right at their middle linebacker, Tim Kearney, and turned back toward me, then used his own judgment to break either left or right. It is a good play, if I am given enough time. And the line gave it to me. My third pass of the game to John, breaking clear to the right took us to the Cardinal 4-yard line. From there, McCutcheon sliced in for the TD on his first try.

This was the way we were meant to play and I was ecstatic, clapping everyone on the back and telling them what a great job they were doing as Tom Dempsey converted to make it Rams 7, Cards 3.

Rod Perry, our speedy little cornerback, got us the ball back almost immediately. He intercepted a Hart pass at the 50 and ran it back to the 35. Now we wanted to show a lust for sixes we had failed to show all season. Lee Bennett sent me in with instructions to reach for Ron Jessie in the end zone. That would have stung the Cardinals, but Ron was well covered by Norm Thompson, who knocked the pass down.

O.K. We'd just have to do it in several bites instead of just one big gulp. On the second down I faded to the left for another pass, then tossed a little shovel pass to John Cappelletti, who was fading to the left with me. He rambled right by their defensive end, who was still going after me—for a gain of 13 yards. Clutch got 9 more on his favorite sweep around right end, with nice blocks by Jessie and Cappelletti. Clutch came right back up the middle for 6 more and a first down on the Card 7.

Kenny Myer wig-wagged yet another option pass to John Cappelletti. That play was going good: why not? The other two passes to John had taken more time to develop. Here, knocking on the Cardinals' goal line, where they had less territory to defend, everything seemed a bit accelerated. I was still backpedaling when John made his move. I kind of thought he'd break, as he had twice before, to his right. He broke left, in toward the middle, and I should have been firing as he made his move. I did throw a split second later, and that was too late. Kearney had recovered, got back into the lane and intercepted in the end zone. Shoot. That was a good call. And I blew a great chance to put us ahead 14–3.

But I wasn't going to let it bother me. I missed that bus. But there'd always be another. It came after we lost some ground on an exchange of punts, and another Bakken field goal.

Third and ten on our own 35. I brought instant joy to a Coliseum crowd of 64,000 when I hit Harold Jackson on a 65-yard touchdown pass. I had great protection. Harold sprinted behind Norm Thompson and then I stepped up into the pocket. That is an eerie feeling. You know there are 250-pound linemen fighting all around you and you're right in the middle of that pounding pit and you can't care about them, you're only worried about your receiver down-field. When Harold got a step or two ahead, I let go. The pass was right on the money, the roar of the crowd told me so and Harold took it going away on the 15. Now we had two TD's on the board.

We should have had another, or at least a field goal. Monte Jackson intercepted a long pass by Jim Hart. I hit Ron Jessie on a good sideline pass to the Ram 45 and, although we only had twenty-six seconds on the clock, we had enough time to get into Tom Dempsey's field goal country. But I overthrew Harold Jackson twice and zipped the ball behind John Cappelletti, who was in the clear. We ran out of downs and punted as the gun sounded, ending the half.

Ron Jessie came off the field with me. He was rubbing his neck. I asked him why. "This guy Reaves has been clobbering me in the back of the neck—after the play is dead and when I'm not looking." Uh huh. Kenny Reaves. One of the league's nice guys. There was an air of restrained exuberance in the locker room at halftime. The offense was moving the ball, the defense had held Hart to six completions out of thirteen attempts. And no touchdowns. We were going to win.

But the third quarter was really weird. Cullen Bryant started things off for us by exploding up the right sideline on the kickoff after a key block by Terry Nelson and shazam! We were ahead 21–6. But the rest of the third quarter was all St. Louis. Hart took the Cards on two sustained drives, one for 67 yards, the other for 87, threw seven out of eight completions, converted on four third down situations, and closed the gap to 21–20 as the quarter ended. Our offensive unit had the ball for only four plays the entire quarter. Against a team such as the Cards were today, the best defense is a good offense. Did we have it? Not in the third quarter we didn't. We had third-quarter troubles at Cincinnati. Now, here, it was the same story.

But we got back on track in the fourth. Starting on our own 26, we moved the ball with a vengeance. John and Clutch ran like bulls, I threw some good passes under the coverage to John and Harold and then, on third and five on the Cardinal 5, I faded back to pass. They had my receivers covered. But they weren't putting any pressure on me. I drifted out of the pocket to my left, saw that Harold had cleared out the left side and calculated the distance to the red flag at the goal line. Shoot, I said, I can make that. At the flag Tim Kearney almost took my head off to make me pay for my hubris. But the ref's hands went up above his

133

head. TD! Normally, I hate showboaters who spike the ball after a touchdown. But my feelings carried me away. I slammed the ball to the turf.

And when Demps made the conversion good and we were ahead 28–20, I thought we had the game well in hand. Could the Cards score twice against our defense in nine minutes? I thought not, but they did. Hart threw four straight completions, to Pat Tilley up the left side for 18 yards, to Ike Harris for 19 yards, to J. V. Cain for 25 yards and a touchdown. And our front four didn't touch him. Instead of dropping back his usual six or seven steps, Hart was taking three steps back and firing fast.

I have never seen a quarterback play a half like this (although I had one myself as a senior at SC when I threw 11 out of 17 completions for 225 yards and four touchdown passes to overcome a 24–6 half-time lead by the great Irish of Notre Dame and beat them 55–24). But I blame myself for letting Hart have another chance. It was our ball with four minutes left. All we had to do was keep it. But by now St. Louis's defense had made all the necessary adjustments to stop our straight-ahead power. Now was the time for some razzmatazz.

But we went straight at them. Sweep to Clutch: 3 yards. Clutch up the middle: no gain. Kenny Myer called our usual third down pass, against a prevent defense that was ready for it. I faded; no one was clear, I scrambled to my left, and had made only about half the yards I needed for the first down when Mark Arneson closed in for the kill. Though I was beyond the line of scrimmage, I faked a running pass and instead of clobbering me, Arneson went high in the air to block the pass. I ducked under him and dashed for the first down marker and a 9-yard gain. Arneson nailed me, but Kenny Reaves came sliding in late. "That's right," he hissed, "break that little bastard's neck." I picked myself up and confronted

Reaves—and said quietly, "Why do you want to break my neck? This is just a game." Reaves looked dumbfounded. He had no answer for me and I turned and trotted back to the huddle.

Then came the most crucial plays of the game. With a little more than two minutes to play, I sent Cappelletti over right tackle. Not a good play here. John got 2 lousy yards. Second and eight. The Cards took time out and I went over to talk to Knox and Myer. I wanted to call a quick draw. Ken wanted me to throw a quick out to Harold Jackson. Knox took Jackson out, put in Terry Nelson as a second tight end and told me to keep the ball myself on a roll-out to the left. Mike Sensibaugh came all the way in from his position at free safety to tackle me for a 2-yard loss.

Two-minute warning. Now what? Another conference with Knox and Myer. We decided on a play action pass to Harold Jackson. But when I came up to the line of scrimmage, I noted they were in nickel defense. I called an audible, a short pass to Clutch under their five-deep-backs' (or "nickel") coverage, which could get us the first down we needed. If we got it, we could kill the clock. I faded to pass. Clutch wasn't open. Neither was anyone else. I couldn't just throw the ball away. I'd already gained 40 yards scrambling. Maybe I could gain 10 more. Or maybe if I scrambled, I'd find somebody breaking late. But, damn it, I didn't. The canny old veteran, Bobby Bell, caught me for an 11-yard loss. My mistake. And a costly one.

Now we had to punt. Rusty Jackson gave the ball a good ride: 47 yards. Only trouble was that Terry Metcalf (who had only gained 3 yards rushing all day on eleven carries) ran the punt back 29 yards to our 48. That was just close enough for Hart to perform his magic. His first two passes got him zilch. Third and ten. Kaboom! A 26-yard comeback pass to Ike Harris put the ball on our 22. Not quite enough for a Jim Bakken field goal. But one more short pass and they would be. That's where Hart crossed us up. After gaining only 14 yards on the ground the entire fourth quarter, he faked the pass and gave the ball to Steve Jones on a draw. That caught us in the wrong coverage and Jones went right by Hacksaw Reynolds for a 14-yard gain to our 8-yard line. With seven seconds on the clock, Bakken kicked for three points and made 'em. Final score: Rams 28–Cards 30.

In the locker room Coach Knox said, "We got a lot of things done, but the only thing we didn't do is win and that's the name of the game." He looked awful. The way our defense had been playing all year, you'd think we could win with twenty-eight points. What a crazy game. Count on nothing. Assume nothing. Play like hell. And even then, you can run up against a guy with a hot hand—and lose.

No. We didn't lose. The Cards won. It's not the end of the world. San Francisco has been losing, too, and we still have a half game on them. Next week, against the 49ers, we will determine who wins our division. That's all there is to it.

Coach Knox was reserved in his praise for my play. But I completed 10 for 17 and 172 yards, 4 for 4 in the pressure of the second half, got the offense on track again and did damn near everything asked of me. There is no way they can not start me against the 49ers at Candlestick Park. But I will still be on trial.

Carroll Rosenbloom phoned me at home this evening to tell me I did well. At first Cindy wouldn't let him talk to me. We'd been having a lot of crank calls. This was just one more. She gave me a look that said, "Why the hell don't we get an unlisted number?"

"No," the voice on the other end said, now slightly nettled, "this *is* Carroll Rosenbloom."

"Oh my gosh!" said Cindy. Making a face, she handed me the phone.

"Hello?"

"Pat," said C.R., "I'm so proud of you. You did everything we asked of you. I'm sorry we didn't win. But you played well, very well. Enjoy your evening."

After that I did. Cindy was mortified and she says she is going to write C.R. a note of apology. But I had Joe Collins and the gang over and we had a fine evening. Just a little red wine and some pizza. But the good friends made it the end of a good day.

November 15

READING THE *Times* WAS AN ENTERTAINMENT—ASIDE FROM Bob Oates' comment that I lost the game yesterday by throwing an interception in the first quarter; he said I forced the pass and that experienced quarterbacks never throw in the middle like that. I do not think Oates remembers all the times that Johnny Unitas and Bart Starr and John Brodie threw the same kind of passes for touchdowns. It is only when somebody picks it off that it is a bad pass.

The delightful thing about this morning's sports page was that it reported one hell of a day yesterday in the NFL. In addition to our barn burner in Los Angeles (which was good old-fashioned pro-football-as-show-business), there were great games all over the league. New England upset Baltimore, Seattle had a near-miss at Minnesota, the New York Giants throttled the Redskins, Atlanta surprised San Francisco, New Orleans edged Detroit by one point. The game is alive and well.

For a change Knox told us today—Monday—who would be starting next Sunday at Candlestick. Me. So, I have a hold on the job. But I think it is a shaky one. All season the coaches have been saying Shack's the best man. So have most of the players, even my best friends on the team, Bob Klein and Rob Scribner. Now I am number one and I do not know what to think about speculation in the press that the decision to make me number one was Carroll Rosenbloom's.

Speculating on the speculation, all I can say to myself is that whoever made the decision—the coaches, C.R., Don Klosterman, or some combination of them all—it is a good one. There's a subtle difference between my quarterbacking and Shack's that can't be measured on any computers. Naturally, I am prejudiced. But I think the San Francisco game will demonstrate that difference. In our first game with San Francisco, Shack wasn't mobile enough and gave up the ball. I am more mobile. And so far I haven't given up the ball.

At our team party this afternoon at El Castillo in Long Beach—tamales, enchiladas, *burritos* and beer—Harold Jackson confided to me that he might not come back next year. He's playing out his option. He feels he is being underutilized. I'd like to help him change his mind about that. If I throw him a few more TD passes and if we go to the Super Bowl, he might see things differently.

November 16

TODAY JOHN WILLIAMS, MY RIGHT TACKLE AND THE GUY who's going to have to keep Tommy Hart off my back Sunday, told Larry Stewart of the *Herald-Examiner,* "All the players know who the quarterback should be. The team is aware who is best."

"Who?" said Stewart.

"I'm not going to make a statement on that," John said.

I am worried.

I esteem John Williams as much as anyone on the squad. He's one of the best blockers on the team and one of the hardest workers. He's a sensitive guy to boot and going into his last year of dental school at the University of Maryland. But I hope he isn't going to start a James Harris fan club. At my expense. I suppose I will not know for sure until about four P.M. Sunday.

November 17

JOHN WILLIAMS CAME UP TO ME BEFORE PRACTICE TODAY and told me he was "misconstrued" in the *Herald-Examiner* yesterday. "Don't pay any attention to newspaper talk," he said. "We're behind you all the way."

I laughed. "I don't want you behind me, John. I want you in front of me, keeping Tommy Hart and Jimmy Webb away from me."

He laughed too. I think everything is going to be all right. I have been very careful to say nothing negative about Shack. The papers continue to quote me as saying that James Harris has proven himself and that I am still working to do so. For his part, Shack has been a big help to me. He could be sulking on the sidelines. Instead, he is always right there at my side, encouraging me, giving me tips and advice. He couldn't be more of a team player here and if helping me helps the team then he will do it.

To counter the 49ers' big rush, the best in the NFL, by all accounts, we're going to use more screen passes, draws, roll-outs and bootlegs. We also think we can blow Ron Jessie and

Harold Jackson by their cornerbacks, Jimmy Johnson, who is thirty-eight, and Bruce Taylor, who isn't the fastest cornerback in our division. But that doesn't mean that we will be throwing a whole lot. Coach Knox has reminded me twelve times this week that Atlanta ran the ball fifty-two times last Sunday to beat the 49ers.

Twenty-one points should beat them. They're not going to score that much on us. And we can score on them. I looked at some reels of our first game against San Francisco. We had four holding penalties in the first quarter—and we overcame three of them to keep driving. That means we can move the ball on them. If we don't hold and if we don't fumble, we're gonna kick their ass.

November 20

SHORT WORKOUT THIS MORNING, THEN WE TOOK OUR charter flight to San Francisco. We ran a little bit at Candlestick shortly after we got off the plane and then hustled in to our hotel to catch what was left of the SC-UCLA game on TV. I bet Scrib ten dollars on the game, each of us taking our own schools, of course.

With Carl Ekern in our darkened room at the Stanford Court (which has got to be the nicest hotel we've seen so far), I watched SC take a 24–0 lead, then phoned to Scrib's room. Deadpan, I said, "Say, Scrib, my TV's not working. You got the SC-UCLA score?" He hung up. I cradled the phone and sat back to enjoy my team's victory. I hate myself at moments like this. Uh, huh. Final score: USC 24–UCLA 14. My successor, Vince Evans, *a black quarterback,* was super. And talk about mobile. He scrambled 36 yards today for SC's final TD to put the game away.

Stanford University fired Coach Jack Christiansen yesterday; and today at Strawberry Canyon his players carried him *on* to the field for his final game against California. His men then went ahead and upset Cal 27–24, to give Christiansen a 5–0 record against the Bears. They say alumni pressure forced Jack out. I wonder: what does a college coach have to do these days to keep his job? I love academia and could be happy for the rest of my life on a good campus where thinking and ideas come first. And I think I could be a good college coach. But never if it involved having to please powerful alumni who'd tell me, "Win or else."

November 21

THE 49ER GAME. I DIDN'T MAKE ANY MISTAKES. I GOT sacked three times in the first quarter alone, once from my blind side by the notorious Tommy Hart. But I didn't give up the ball. I hung in there. Our screens and draws didn't work. Nothing worked.

But nothing was working for Jim Plunkett either. The only difference was, he was being booed by the ignorant 49er fans as early as his first series—and I wasn't being booed (because *our* ignorant fans were back in L.A., watching on TV). That made it easier on me. And harder on Jim, one of the nicest guys that ever put on a helmet, and a helluva good passer to boot. With a little advance preparation by the home-town writers, maybe the fans would have realized what kind of a game this was going to be—a real defensive battle between the two best defensive teams in either league.

141

I have never seen defensive play like this. We made 32 yards rushing in the first half, the 49ers 27. We got 56 yards passing to their 35. We punted seven times, they six. It wasn't that either Plunkett or I was bad. The defenses were just that damned good.

For instance, in the second quarter, a Tom Wittum punt took a funny bounce near our goal line and Jim Bertelsen tried to block to keep them from downing it inside the 5. The ball hit him in the leg and the 49ers recovered on our 3. But our defense dug in. They held Delvin Williams to 2 yards in three power plays. Williams had been burning up the league: he rushed for 194, 180 and 88 yards in his last three games. He got a total of 9 yards all day against Ray Malavasi's shock troops. And here, the Niners had to settle for a field goal by Steve Mike-Mayer. After that they never got closer than our 31-yard line. That was late in the game and when they did so, our defense was affronted. Retaliating, Butch Robertson threw Scott Bull for a 10-yard loss. And then Rod Perry intercepted Bull and ran the ball back 43 yards. So there.

Our guys seemed to be picking up fumbles and intercepting their passes all afternoon. In the second quarter Jim Youngblood made an interception at midfield to give us the break we needed. On the very next play I threw a 60-yard pass to Ron Jessie. He wasn't my primary receiver, but—nice surprise—I had some extra time and when I saw Harold Jackson was double covered, I threw it high and long to Jessie. I didn't know if he was open. I just threw him a bomb and hoped he'd make a star of me. He was open, though, and caught the ball pedaling backward, hanging onto it tight as he landed on his butt.

Those were all the points we really needed to win. But we got two more touchdowns and a field goal in the second half and we won the big one 23–3. Monte Jackson intercepted one of Plunkett's flat passes in the third quarter and returned it 41 yards to ice the game; and he grabbed off another later. Now he's leading the league in interceptions.

With support like that, we didn't have to show much offense, as Coach Knox had insisted all week. I was proudest, however, when, leading only 9–3 in the third quarter, after having flubbed a chance to score from the San Francisco 26 on a turnover, we got the ball right back on another fumble at the San Francisco 35 and punched it in for a TD in seven running plays.

From up in the press box Coach Lee Bennett suggested we go into the Power-I. This is a formation where Lawrence McCutcheon gets the ball a good deal farther back from the line and then is able to pick his own hole, running wherever he sees daylight. It is a formation that has been run to best effect through the years by USC—by O. J. Simpson, Clarence Davis, A. D. Davis and Ricky Bell. Lee's idea was inspired. With Bob Klein and Doug France making some good blocks, we ran Clutch four straight times to daylight for 29 yards. John Cappelletti got 5 more. And then I sneaked it in from the 1 for the TD. Moving the ball on the ground like that, we didn't have to pass. And, not having to pass, we didn't run the risk of losing yardage (and the ball itself) on sacks. I ended up the day with a mere three for eight completions. Heroes? The entire defense—and their Coach Ray Malavesi.

As defensive coordinator Ray calls every coverage from the sideline, wig-wagging to Hack Reynolds just as Ken Myer does to me. We have thirteen basic coverages and four variations off each one, so Ray's job is not a simple one. But the players have complete faith in what he tells them. "Our entire defense plays as a coordinated unit," I have heard Jack Youngblood say. "If everybody just does what Ray tells 'em, we'll win." Malavesi was a star lineman under Red Blaik at Army in 1950 and he coached at Minnesota and Memphis

State and Wake Forest, the Hamilton Tiger-Cats (in the Canadian League), then the Buffalo Bills, the Denver Broncos and the Oakland Raiders before he landed in L.A.

Ray is a warm, gregarious guy; because he works with the defense, I do not know him as well as I'd like to. But I know one thing: his players would walk to their next game on their knees if he asked them to, no questions.

After the game I was mobbed, by kids on the field and the press. Paul Hornung interviewed me on the field for CBS, then the kids swarmed me. I gave my chin strap to one, waist towel to another, wrist wrap to a third, the other wrist wrap to a fourth. Then I ran for the locker room and was ambushed by another reporter. By the time I got to the locker area I was way late for Knox's wrapup. "Excuse me, please," I said to the reporters crowded around the door, waiting. "You mind if I get in here?"

The writers smiled and opened their ranks like the Red Sea and cheered my move with some sarcasm. I'd been forcing my way into the 49er locker room and one of the home-town scribes said, "Come in, come in, by all means. We need a quarterback all right." I blushed and finally found our locker room about two hundred feet away.

Coach Knox was happiest about our third quarter. Instead of losing then, as we had in our two previous outs, we outscored our enemy 17–0.

I was the last guy out of the locker room. I hadn't done that much, but the press wanted me. The San Francisco writers, looking for something bright to write for the home-town fans, wanted to know what I thought of the Niners' rush. "They *have* a rush," I said, understating it by about 1000 percent. "I have some mighty fine guys protecting me. Anybody gets by them—they gotta be good."

When I got out of the locker area I found a girl waiting

for me. She was Betty Cuniberti, a reporter for the *Chronicle*, who wasn't allowed inside; she wanted to talk about reported dissension on the team. I told her to wait a moment and shouted to Jack Geyer, "Would you make sure the bus doesn't leave without me?" Geyer, one of our great p.r. guys, rolled his eyes. "Oh, you can bet *that* won't happen." Then I turned to Ms. Cuniberti and told her there was no dissension. "We're all professionals," I said. "We just worry about ourselves. We can't worry about what's happening to others."

In the San Francisco Airport we learned our jet wasn't ready. With war whoops we marched toward one of the terminal's alcove bars just as a very sexy blonde was emerging. Two of our finest and strongest picked the lady up and took her back into the alcove, set her on the bar and bought her a drink. She was not unwilling. She wore an orange jersey halter top cut to the navel and she was enjoying the fuss, the hooting and the hollering and the cat cries.

Then Coach Knox arrived on the scene. Knox is from Puritan Scotch-Irish stock and, most of the time, even his hair is clenched. The players fell back, a little like kids caught with their hands in the cookie jar. But Knox was loose as a goose now. Laughing, he grabbed the blonde by the shoulders and buried his face in her bosom. She loved it.

Then the others started shouting, "Bring on the rook. Get the rook. Where's the rook?" There are seven other rookies on the team, but I knew they weren't asking for Dwight Scales or Pat Thomas or even Rusty Jackson, who had had a fine day punting against a big rush. They wanted me to come up and emulate my coach. I swaggered up through the crowd, blushing furiously, and, accompanied by bawdy shouts of approval, I did what Knox had done. A salacious scene? No. It was all in good fun. No harm, no foul. More important to me, then, was the significance of the whole tableau: I had arrived. Now it wasn't just Carroll Rosenbloom who wanted me, or the coaches who wanted me. Now the team wanted me.

November 23

DAY OFF TODAY, TUESDAY. IT HAS BEEN A TOUGH SEASON for Cindy, too. I know I am not paying her enough attention. But tonight we will go out to dinner and then on to see *Chorus Line* at the Shubert in Century City. I will be with Cindy when I can. What more can I do? I never thought playing pro football would be such an all-consuming thing. Maybe it doesn't have to be. This is my rookie season—and a very weird, up-and-down season at that.

November 25

CRITICS' CORNER. BOB OATES IN THE *Times:*

Haden is still very much a rookie. . . . His promise does seem to be excellent. He throws at least one bomb a game, he's a leader, and he has the poise not to give the ball away, but you can't make even a Rhodes scholar into an NFL quarterback overnight.

What do I have to do to get a good review from Oates?
Jeff Weir in *Pro Football West* worries about Rusty Jackson's "extra step punting [that] might eventually carry the Rams out of the playoffs," ham-handed punt receiving by

Cullen Bryant and Jim Bertelsen and Tom Dempsey's shaky performances on the tries for extra points. Weir writes:

> Perhaps the Rams' special teams' members ought to reconsider their roles, for L.A.'s long-term playoff chances might well fade on a misplaced punt, an errant extra point, or a muffed return. Strong Super Bowl contenders cannot afford such lapses. . . .

Dan Jenkins in *Sports Illustrated:*

> Pat Haden, a young man who looks as though he invented breakfast cereal . . . had to improvise. When the Rams' pocket had collapsed in last month's debacle, Harris was sacked 10 times. This time Haden escaped, and suddenly he sailed the football about 60 yards to Ron Jessie in the San Francisco end zone.

He quoted Don Klosterman, who was with Jenkins up in the press box during the game. "You can't beat good vision," said Don. Then he quoted an anonymous Ram:

> It's been psychologically tough on us not knowing who the quarterback is. If the team were to vote, Harris would get the most votes, and Coach Knox knows this. That's why he's been slow to make the change. But we all like Pat. He's a great kid. For a while there, we just wished the season would get over with. But with the playoffs in view now, I think you'll see us become the kind of football team we're capable of being.

Jenkins added: "If Pat Haden is the quarterback, of course."

November 27

THE TROJANS WERE FLAT TODAY AGAINST NOTRE DAME IN the Coliseum (probably letting down after their emotional win last week against UCLA), and lucky to win it, 17–13. It was my first SC game of the year, the only time when I have been free to see them play.

During halftime, ABC's Jim Lampley had me down on the field for a feature on their national telecast called "The Way It Was"—for nostalgia fans. He showed highlights of our fifty-five-point second half against Notre Dame in 1974. I had a hot hand that day. Almost like the night I threw five touchdown passes for Bishop Amat, all to John McKay, against the number two team in Southern California, Mater Dei. Once that night I tried to throw out of bounds, deliberately, and the wind blew it back in and right into John's hands as he stood in the end zone—right between three defenders.

November 28

THE COACHES HAVE BEEN COMPLAINING THAT THE DEFENSE has been doing most of the work. True. So far they've been carrying the club. Against New Orleans today, however, it was the offense's turn. We had the ball for thirty-nine minutes, eighteen seconds of the game; the Saints for twenty minutes, forty-two seconds.

The game ended up a laugher, 33–14. But we started slow. In the first quarter I flubbed some third down plays, threw an interception into the end zone and we got a mere two field goals, six points, to match the Saints' seven (on a 51-yard TD run by the fine rookie, Chuck Muncie). We were scoring threes instead of sixes. Aargh.

We finally meshed in the second quarter and scored three times, sixes, that is, not threes, showing the kind of manic goal line fever we'd been lacking for most of the year. We drove 89 yards in ten plays for our first TD. The big play was a reverse to Ron Jessie off our familiar McCutcheon sweep to the right. Every good play has to have a counter run off it occasionally. The counter catches the defense napping; and it also sets up the regular play next time you call it. This reverse was good for 22 yards. We got the ball next time when Jack Youngblood forced a fumble on the Saints 34, and five plays later we were in the end zone again, mainly on Clutch's running—including a 19-yard run on a sweep to the right! I tossed him a short pass in the end zone for the score. Third time, after our defense had backed the Saints to their 1-yard line and Cullen Bryant returned their punt to the 19, I threw a pass to Bob Klein for another TD. Bob made a great diving catch in the end zone with a defender hanging around his neck. There's nothing like putting another big marker up on the board with only seconds left in the half. I could imagine Hank Stram figuring he'd be going into the locker room only twelve points behind. Two touchdowns away we're still reachable. But 26–7! I think that might have taken most of the faith, hope and charity out of the Saints.

None of us got too excited about the second half. At half-time, we found Shack stretched out on a table in the training room; then they sent him off to the hospital with a virus. Shack is going through a lot of stress these days. He is worried. He doesn't want to play for the Rams next year, but he isn't sure that anybody else will want him after what has happened to him here. There's not a hell of a lot that any of us can do about that, except worry. And we do. So all we did in the second half was play hard enough to win, 33–14.

Coach Knox gave game balls to Clutch, who passed the 1,000-yard mark for the season with 119 yards on twenty-five carries today, to Merlin Olsen, who tied a record for number of games played as a Ram (206), and to me. They should have cut the seams on the ball and given me one panel, or a fourth of it, I only played well in one quarter, the second.

But Clutch and Ole played well in every quarter. They always do.

For our glamour runner, a guy who has rushed for 1,000 or more each of his three seasons on the Rams and is now the second leading ball carrier in Rams history (next to Dick Bass), Lawrence McCutcheon gets far less ink than he deserves. The press, I guess, takes him for granted.

I take him for granite. I do not understand how he can carry the ball for twenty rushes a game, catch a half dozen passes besides, make as many blocks as he does and take the hits he does from 260-pound linemen and 230-pound linebackers—and still come back next game to do it all again. Yes. I do understand. He is strong. He is determined. And he does not waste any energy getting himself all riled up.

Clutch almost never made it out of Plainview, Texas, where he grew up and played high school ball. He got a football scholarship to Colorado State but wandered back home within weeks. College was too difficult, he said. His mother told him the alternative—chopping cotton alongside his ten brothers and sisters—was (and would be) even more difficult. "Go back to school," she said. "You won't be sorry." So far, Clutch hasn't been. He finished school, drives a nice car, dates the prettiest girls and, at twenty-six, still has a flossy

150

career in football ahead of him. I am glad he listened to his mother.

November 29

Mal Florence's piece about Coach Hank Stram this morning in the *Times* focused more on fashion than it did on football. Mal described Stram's outfit—a cream-colored jacket with brown pocket flaps and matching brown slacks and loafers—and said Stram is the best dressed man in pro football. He'll have to go a good ways to top some of the Rams, who spend big bucks on threads.

I am comfortable in Levis and a sweater, but I am under some pressure to get some new clothes myself. Ron and Shack tell me I'd better start looking like an NFL quarterback; they say I'm entirely too casual and could bring down quarterback standards all over the league, that I ought to invest in some elevator shoes and some mod jackets and slacks. In fact, Ron says I ought to get rid of my Pinto, too. "An NFL quarterback ought to drive a Cadillac," he says, "and have a woman in every town." I pretend to take him seriously and try to consult with him every day on my plans to change from a caterpillar into a butterfly. "Maybe," I told Ron today, "I ought to get a Mercedes instead of a Caddy. . . ." (Ron, of course is all parade and no circus. He himself drives a Hornet station wagon and is devoted to his wife, Liz, and daughter, Joleen, who is a year old.)

But seriously, I do not want to start living on what I am making now on each game. Anything can happen to me at any time. I might hurt my knee or suffer some other injury.

151

And then, if I am not playing and trying to get through law school, I could be a penurious student again.

In the Florence piece, Stram had some nice things to say about me. Mal reminded him that a rookie quarterback hasn't led a team to the NFL championship round since Bob Waterfield did it with the old Cleveland Rams in 1945. Stram said, "Haden is gaining confidence with every game and he should be very tough by the time of the playoffs. Haden has tremendous poise and an awareness of what is happening. Most young quarterbacks have difficulty finding a secondary receiver. They've predetermined who they're going to throw to and, if the man isn't open, they get nervous feet and start to dance. But Haden can pick up the secondary receiver."

I had my father-in-law, Bud Grier, and about a dozen of my closest friends over tonight to help me root for the Vikings against the 49ers on "Monday Night Football." Beer and pizza and a lot of noise. A 49er loss tonight would have clinched the division title for us. I didn't get much help from my friends, who were rooting for the underdogs and insisting that it would be better for the Rams to win it on their own. And I didn't get much help from the Vikings, who lost to the Niners, 20–16. The Vikes stopped neither Wilbur Jackson nor Delvin Williams, who got more than 300 yards between them. What this tells me is that if we meet the Vikings in the playoffs, we can run on them, too.

P. S. Joe Collins won our pool tonight.

P. P. S. And Cindy gave us hell along about one A.M. for making too much noise. She's got the flu and wishes tonight that my friends and I would drop dead.

November 30

CRITICS' CORNER. DOUG KRIKORIAN WRITES IN THE *Examiner* that Coach Knox is shedding his conservative image. He noted we passed nine times Sunday on first down, and that we ran a reverse to Jessie, also on first down. I do not think Doug understands that we passed on first down because we thought they'd be looking for the run. That's all. Coach Knox is not as conservative as many writers think. He'll try whatever works. And if it works, he'll try it again.

Bob Oates has a labored piece in the *Times,* full of surmises about the quarterback situation on the Rams. I wonder why he doesn't come around sometime and talk to us. We never see him, but he cranks out analyses several times a week. He writes that I *seem* to have the starting job because I am "more likely than the others to win pro football's big season-ending games—if not this year, then next year, or some year."

But then Oates goes on: "If Haden can't do it in the next few winters, the club will get someone who can. No one in the organization is making any such statements but the conclusions of club executives can be deduced from what's happened." In other words, Rams policies have to be pieced together by deep thinkers, like the journalists who write on the Kremlin or Peking. Or the Vatican.

More Oates: "It seems evident now that what the Rams think they need [to get to the Super Bowl] . . . is a quarterback like Staubach, Tarkenton or Bob Griese." But, shoot, how many years have these guys played and how few times have they gotten to the Super Bowl? Tarkenton has played in the NFL sixteen years and, so far, he's been in the finals twice. Staubach, an eight-year veteran, has been there twice and Bob Griese, in the league ten years, has made it three times. I guess I don't mind sportswriters who come across more like theater critics than sportswriters. They add something to the game. I just wish they wouldn't use such spurious standards of quarterback worth. Getting to the Super Bowl isn't the only one. Not in this crazy game where the farther you go the more your success depends on the breaks.

December 1

I GOT A PHONE CALL FROM MY AGENT, CHUCK BARNES, THIS morning telling me there is a good chance he can arrange for me to do an American Express commercial over in Oxford. And maybe get an assignment from ABC-TV to do color commentary on the Irish Derby. Just some of the frosting that an NFL quarterback can put on his cake, especially if he plays in either New York or L.A.

That cake and that frosting should last for at least three more years, according to a gal named Lisa Megan Morrow, an astrologer trying to put together a syndicated column on athletes and astrology. Lisa's charted John Cappelletti and Jerry Wilcox, and they both say she's good. She met me at Blair Field after practice and when we took a seat in the stands I told her I didn't believe in astrology. She said she didn't either, but that sometimes the charts "made sense." She said that after studying my "aspects" and Shack's in September she predicted I'd take the job away from him. "Hmmmm," I said, "tell me more."

She said I had Venus and Mars together in Pisces. So?

"That means you're a charmer. No matter how old you get, even if you lose your hair and your teeth fall out, you'll always draw people to yourself." She asked me what I wanted to do after football. I told her maybe go into law and then be dictator of the United States. For a moment she thought I was serious, then laughed and said that, astrologically speaking, I'd be a good politician. "Your mind works conservatively. You won't take too many wild chances. You do better in concrete things, rather than the abstract. And you won't open your mouth when you shouldn't. January twenty-third. You're an Aquarian. That's good. There are *no* Sagittarian politicians!"

I told her I thought she was pretty much on the mark about me. During this entire quarterback controversy, I had had to be a consummate politician. If I'd been anything other than Humble Harve, the quiet rookie, I could have triggered the damnedest dissension anybody ever saw. But I didn't force anyone to take sides.

After the interview with Lisa, somebody showed me a clipping from Hank Hollingsworth's column in the Long Beach *Press-Telegram,* which told me that I must be doing something else right. Hank had an extensive quote from Doug France, our second-year tackle from Ohio State. France is big (six five, 260)—and he's black:

> Haden may be a young quarterback, but he has the poise of an old pro, and he knows how to say the right things at the right time. Nobody ever really pays much attention to the offensive line, unless it makes mistakes, but Haden makes his line feel good. He'll say, "Way to go, line," after he completes a pass or one of the running backs makes a gain.
>
> Or he'll say, "You're doing fine, we'll get 'em next time," if the play doesn't go so well. The point is that Haden always says something to make his line personnel feel good. Today, when McCutcheon made a real good gain, Haden came up to me and

said, "Thanks for opening that big hole!" Man, I felt 10 feet high. Imagine that kid thanking me for opening a hole! That's my job, but Haden made me feel like I had just done something extra special. You want to break your neck for a guy like that.

Sometimes I think I do not need to read anything about myself or the Rams in the papers. I'll read a carping column by Oates and resolve to read no more. Then somebody shows me a column like this one and I am hooked again.

A comment like Doug's makes me feel good because it is strong evidence to me that, despite all the potential for disharmony on the team this year, the Rams are still together. And being together, as a team, is one of the things that makes football so enjoyable. I do not enjoy it, for example, when Shack and Ron start teeing off (as they did this morning at breakfast) on the Rams' inability to "turn the offense loose."

I, too, feel that we ought to be a little ballsier on offense— that we shouldn't even think of "nursing a lead" unless there are only seconds left to play. But grousing about our game strategies among ourselves at breakfast is not the way to change things and it is a good way to destroy the unity that ought to prevail between players and their coach.

What we can do is prove to Knox through our actions on the field that the offense is capable of scoring any time, from any place, moving the ball and keeping it. That means not fumbling and not throwing interceptions. We cannot prove we can do this overnight. But it is worth doing little by little. And we can give Knox some input on the sideline during those time-outs that always seem to come at crucial moments in the game. I am less able to prevail on a play call at the sideline now than I will be in the future. As a rookie I generally keep my eyes and ears open and my mouth closed. But gradually I hope to have more of a say in the calling of plays. And sometime call my own game.

In the meantime I will do what I can. And I will try not

156

to let Shack and Ron weigh me down with their negativism about our offense.

December 2

WE HAD A GOOD OFFENSIVE PRACTICE TODAY. THOUGH THE Atlanta Falcons have beaten a couple of good teams in the past few weeks (San Francisco and Dallas), they should be no problem—less of a problem for us now than they were in our season's opener down South. The reason is that our offense is jelling. As Tom Mack says: "Our timing goes out the window when a different quarterback is in there every week. You don't know whether the quarterback is going to step up or back or out. Now, the line knows how to react and the results are showing."

Tom, our offensive left guard, is talking about his unit, the offensive line, a group that has less experience in the league than most of the other playoff contenders. Doug France and Dennis Harrah are starters this year for the first time. They have come along very fast. But even as offensive linemen, they have the most demanding (and most underrated) jobs in the game. It all takes time and experience. Of course, this year they are getting precisely that. Wait till next year! If only we can keep Tom Mack. Tom feels that playing much longer (he is now in his eleventh year) is going to hold back his progress with the Bechtel Corporation. I would never tell him what to do. But selfishly I would like him to stay one more year, until Greg Horton and Jackie Slater can get a little more experience. Slater (six four, 252 and only twenty-two years old) is going to be a good one. At the College All-Star game, Coach Ara Parseghian said he'd be playing in the Pro

Bowl in a year or two. What little action he has seen this year
tends to bear out Parseghian.

December 4

WHAT CAN YOU SAY ABOUT OUR BEATING ATLANTA 59–0—
an all-time high for the Rams. Everything worked for us. I
wasn't particularly sharp, but even so, passed for 214 yards.
Nothing worked for them. Our defense never let the Falcons
cross midfield. I felt sorry for Pat Peppler, the Falcon general
manager, who had to take over as coach in midseason. Nobody likes to lose like this. But shoot, how do you hold the
score down when even the youngest kids on the team are
playing like vets? On one 80-yard bomb Dwight Scales looked
like a Harold Jackson or a Ron Jessie. Why were we passing
late in the game? Two reasons: 1) they were blitzing on us—
inviting us to throw the bombs, and 2) according to the
league's complicated playoff formulae, the more points we
score today the better chance we have of getting the home
field advantage if we meet the Vikings in the playoffs.

We were loose today and I think we play better that way.
I knew it was going to be fun on our first drive: I completed
my first three passes, 16 yards to Klein, 22 yards to Cappelletti, 17 yards to Jackson. By the end of the half we were
just entertaining the 57,000 who showed up. Our last play
of the half was a triple reverse with me on the end of it—at
which point I tossed a pass to McCutcheon for all of a 6-yard
gain. By the time I came out of the game, early in the third
quarter, we were ahead 31–0 and we had scored every time
we got the ball—though some of those scores were field goals

and could have been TD's if I'd thrown a couple of balls just a little bit better.

The Rams fans (are they a sadistic bunch?) loved all of it. Their roars only got louder as the score rose. Maybe some of them remembered the last championship team the Rams ever had, the '51 team, an offensive dynamo that racked up scores of 54–14, 48–21, 45–21, 42–17 and 42–14. How, on this day, could they *not* remember? Most of the members of that team were here for their twenty-fifth reunion in the Coliseum: Norm Van Brocklin, Bob Waterfield, Tom Fears, Crazylegs Hirsch, Deacon Dan Towler, Tank Younger. John Ramsey, the Coliseum announcer, introduced them all at half-time. And you know what I was thinking when I came back on the field and saw them all standing around the Rams' bench? That when these guys beat the Cleveland Browns for the championship in 1951, I wasn't even born yet.

After the game Paul Hornung got me and Larry McCutcheon on CBS in a sideline interview, and then I ran back up the track and into the tunnel past quite a few hundred fans who stayed to cheer me. A good feeling. After my shower it took me a half hour to get from the locker room door to my car: lots of people, mostly kids, wanted my autograph and the Coliseum had to provide me with two bodyguards.

December 5

TOM DEMPSEY MISSED HIS FIRST THREE POINT-AFTER-TD attempts yesterday. Today he and Rich Saul, center, and Steve Preece, holder, were out on Blair Field early, practicing conversions.

I really empathize with Demps. So frequently, a blocked

kick isn't his fault. And yet he takes the rap for it. That's got to be frustrating, especially for a guy who has made it big in the NFL despite an absolutely unique handicap. How many others have done what Tom has—with a right arm and a right leg withered from birth? None.

And how many others in the league can stand up to a bar and match him pitcher for pitcher? Darn few, I would imagine. And that is a record I feel Demps is proud of, too. I like Tom. At training camp he was hard on me and once razzed me right out of Me and Ed's Pizza Parlor where he and Bertelsen and Brooks and Jaworski drank beer every night before supper, just on the grounds that I was a rookie. Now, however, he couldn't be a better friend. And he's been pleading with me to join him and the gang on Friday nights when we are in town for sessions of beer drinking and skeet shooting.

December 6

CRITICS' CORNER. WHICH DAY'S *Times* D'YA READ? BOB OATES in *yesterday's Times:* "The Rams have lately seemed to be putting things together, growing in confidence with Haden. It's too early yet to tell about that young man but he hasn't done many things wrong." Bob Oates in *today's Times.* "So, after their midseason slump, the Rams are getting better, and much of their improvement can probably be traced to their new leader, Pat Haden. . . . They have given the ball away only four times on fumbles in Haden's last four games as a starter and only three times on interceptions, a total of seven. By contrast, in the four games before that, they turned it over 14 times on nine fumbles and five interceptions."

Tonight, on "Monday Night Football," in full view of Howard Cosell and Alex Karras and Frank Gifford and God and everybody, pro football gained an extra measure of respect. The Oakland Raiders beat the Cincinnati Bengals convincingly when it might have made more sense for them to take it easy and lose. They already have a playoff berth and have sewn up all home field advantages. A win by the Bengals tonight would have eliminated the Steelers, who have allowed only two touchdowns in their last eight games. Now the Raiders will probably have to meet the Steelers in the playoffs, a team everyone says will go all the way. Coach John Madden is a hell of a guy. He had nothing to lose by losing, but plenty to lose by winning. And he won.

December 7

THOUGH WE'VE CLINCHED A PLACE IN THE PLAYOFFS (WITH a fourth-straight division championship for Chuck Knox in four years), winning the Detroit game Saturday night in Pontiac may mean a home field advantage for us on December 19. So we'd better win. But Detroit will be tough. The Lions have only lost one of their last seven games at home. And they've got the blitzingest, doggingest team in the league. They don't have that good a defense; they try to make up for it by rushing the passer, sometimes with nine, even ten men. Coach Knox, who used to coach at Detroit, says, "They will throw more dogs and blitzes at us in this one game than we've seen all season combined."

That's a threat. But it's a challenge, too. I could easily end up throwing a couple of bombs to Jackson and Jessie right away and the game would be over early.

Barbara Hunter of NBC News, a woman who has chosen to zero in on the sports world for her network and is very damn knowledgeable, interviewed me after practice for "The Today Show." She and her two-man crew took me to the beach not far from Blair Field, where, at sunset, we kicked our shoes off and strolled along, chatting about my rookie season with the Rams, Oxford and life in general. I think it was a good interview because she drew out of me just exactly what I thought needed saying.

Then my brother Jim and I went to a Long Beach bar for a drink. I was going to go out and help him buy a car, but we realized we didn't have time for that today: I had to be down in Orange County at seven P.M. for an athletic banquet at Tustin High School. There aren't enough hours in the day anymore. I will be glad to get back to Oxford again where Cindy and I will have some time to ourselves.

December 9

WE ARRIVED IN DETROIT TOO LATE TO GO ANYWHERE FOR a decent dinner. But we ordered some oyster stew at a bar across the road from the Kingsley Inn in Pontiac, had a few beers and listened to some music, then plowed through the snow and across the icy highway back to our rooms.

Some of the guys seemed a little morose tonight. I guess it *would* be more fun to be home instead of alone in this— motel. But the season will be over soon. If we go all the way, only three more games after this.

Even during the season we have our good times. Tuesday night Bob Klein and Joanne, Rob Scribner and Jennifer, and Cindy and I went to Ma Maison together in L.A. Carroll

162

Rosenbloom insists each of us go out for dinner once during the season and charge it to him. Like everyone else, we didn't scrimp or scant on C.R.'s offer. We had some very nice French wines at strategic times during dinner. And the tab came to $266.33 plus tip.

One of our fringe benefits. On the other hand, as Rams, we sometimes have extraordinary expenses. For example, Bill Simpson had to fork over nine hundred dollars on the plane tonight to Mickey Ducich, our film (and utility) man, for ninety tickets to the game Saturday night. Bill's from Royal Oak and he has a lot of friends and relatives here who want to see him play. Most of them probably think he gets his tickets free. He doesn't. He has to pay face value for them, just like everybody else.

December 10

WE WORKED OUT BRIEFLY TODAY AT THE PONTIAC STADIUM. It's a building with a soft fiber glass dome supported by air and, of all the new domed stadiums, it is the only one that came in under its original budget of $55 million. The only trouble with it is the playing surface. It is some kind of artificial turf on top of concrete and loose sand. It's got waves in it and I do not like it. And when you look up, the lights get you right in the eyes.

Soon as we returned to the motel, about three P.M., a lot of the players hustled across the road for some serious drinking. (We have a rule that no player may be seen in the bar of a hotel we're staying in.) Some of the guys stayed there almost until our team meeting began at nine o'clock. Needless to say, they were weaving a little when they got to the meeting and I am surprised they made it back safe across the highway. Oh well, they have a long time to sleep it off tomorrow because this is another one of those late games, a nine P.M. affair with Howard, Alex and Frank at the controls upstairs. So far we haven't shown their Monday night audiences our best. Two losses: S.F. and Cincinnati. Maybe the third time's the charm.

Ironic thing about this game—and it's being carried by all the press wires—is that James Harris is leading the NFC this week in passing and he'll be sitting on the bench tomorrow. He has a rating of 94.7 under a complicated formula that measures percent of touchdowns, interceptions and completions per pass attempt, plus average yards per pass. Actually, I have a higher rating than Shack, 97.0, but I've only thrown 100 times so far this season. Shack has thrown 141, just one more than he needs to qualify for the NFC title. I have to throw 40 times tomorrow to qualify. I'll be lucky to throw half that many.

December 12

COACH KNOX WAS RIGHT. THE LIONS CAME RIGHT AT ME, dogging, blitzing. I called the right audibles at the line—and overthrew Ron Jessie twice on long, long passes that had touchdown written on them. The ball, as Shack had warned me before the game, sailed inside this stadium. It was like playing indoors.

And then I was out of the game. On that last throw to Jessie my right foot got caught in the lovely Astroturf. One Lion hit me high, another low, and I went down with them in a twisting heap. I tried playing on my throbbing knee for another series, then took myself out of the game. Shack went in for me and I huddled with Doctor Kerlan. Goddamn! We didn't even need this game, it didn't mean a damn thing because the Vikings had drubbed the Dolphins earlier in the afternoon. And now, with a week to go before the playoffs in Dallas, I was hurt.

They took me to our locker room in a little kiddie car that looked like an oversize Detroit Lions helmet and I sat there feeling very sorry for myself while Gie Giemont helped me off with my shoulder pads and started getting an ice bag ready for my knee. My mind was a jumble of thoughts and my mood went from somber to sanguine to somber again.

"If there's any way," I told Gie, "I'll be playing against Dallas." A moment later I said to myself: "Oh, hell, they'll never let me play against Dallas."

Dr. Kerlan told me on the bench that he'd open up the knee tomorrow and look inside it. That'll be just super. I told him I wanted another opinion before he cut on anything and he shot me an angry look.

Gie said, "Let me tell you one thing, Pat. We've got the best people in the world to work on it."

"Shoot," I said, "I won't *be* here. I go to England on January twelfth." Then I realized: there'd probably be no skiing for me this year. And I was really planning on that.

It didn't sound to me as if anything good was happening to the Rams out on the field. I heard cheers from the stands and then a long, sustained roar. Somebody came in and said the Lions were on the Rams 5 after a 47-yard pass play. Gie put an ice bag on my knee and wrapped a big Ace bandage around it, then went back out to the tunnel to see what was happening. "Find a radio," I told him, "if you can."

While he was gone, I sat there alone in the fluorescent glare of this oversize room listening to another big roar from the partisan Lions rooters. And then another. When Gie came back in, just before halftime intermission, he said the score was Lions 17, Rams 3. Dandy.

When I got back out to the bench after the intermission, on crutches, I watched the Rams put together almost as good a third quarter as we'd had all year. Using Phillips, Bertelsen and Bryant (Knox was taking no chances on John or Clutch getting hurt), Shack led us to two touchdowns and a field goal.

And there we were in the lead. It was a nice comeback. But we didn't get any more points. And neither did the Lions. By the end of the game most of the rooters had long cleared out of the stadium. They didn't like stutter, flutter, fumble and fall football—which is what both teams were playing late in the game.

We had a subdued plane ride home. I was manic. I was sure they were going to operate on me tomorrow—and that I could kiss this season and maybe the next good-bye. And even if they didn't operate, I was convinced Shack would get the starting role in Dallas.

Dr. Kerlan came by and told me exactly what was going to happen. "We'll take you to Centinela Hospital when we get to L.A.," he said. "It'll be about four in the morning. Then, sometime tomorrow, Clarence Shields and I will perform an arthroscopy." I raised an eyebrow. "We have this little flexible fiber optic," he explained. "We make a little incision on the side of your knee—you'll be under total anesthesia, so it won't hurt a bit. We introduce a light source into the fiber optic and we'll be able to look all around inside the knee. If there isn't too much damage in there, we'll just pull out and go home. If there's a lot of damage we'll operate then and there. If there's a cast on your knee when you wake up, you'll know we operated. If there isn't, you may be O.K."

"O.K. enough to play?" I asked. "Against Dallas?"

He looked at me lugubriously, half bent over with his own

painful arthritis. He is a guy who knows what pain is. Then he smiled. "Maybe," he said. "Maybe."

Tom Mack and Bob Klein and Rich Saul all tried to cheer me up. Tom said everybody had had knee injuries. Most of them weren't serious. He predicted I'd play. Klein, who'd gotten injured a year ago in the same stadium, agreed with Mack.

I told them I wasn't so sure. "And if I don't play against Dallas, what kind of future do I have with the Rams? I've had all the breaks I'm gonna get. If I lose the starting job once more, I've had it."

Then Steve Rosenbloom came by. I had a three-across seat to myself and Steve sat in the middle seat, so he could talk quietly to me. "There's no way we want you to play against Dallas unless you're O.K." he said. "But if you can't play, don't worry. You're still our guy. You've got a big future with us."

Uh huh, I said to myself. I am very gloomy right now—about everything. Life is going on all around me. In the back of the plane the cowboys are playing their country and western music and drinking their Coors. In front of me, the scouts are busy with their charts, and the clackety-clack of a few typewriters tells me that some of the reporters are hard at work on stories they will be filing as soon as we land in L.A.

Across the aisle, however, Butch Robertson is bending a newcomer's ear. He is Larry Merchant, a former sports columnist for the *New York Post,* who is now working for NBC Sports. Butch is telling Merchant (in about twenty thousand well-chosen words) about his philosophy of excellence. "I took fifteen rejects for my Little League team," he is saying. "Some of those kids had the right shoe on the left foot and the left shoe on the right foot, but I turned 'em all around. I taught 'em to have pride. I told 'em nobody would play for me unless they made their beds in the morning—and I made sure their mothers knew about that, too. Pretty soon,

167

I had those kids believing they had to win. And they did win. . . ." I dozed off for a time. When I woke, Butch was still talking to Merchant. "Now, I believe in life, takin' in all the experiences life has to offer. Now I come to L.A. out of Southern U. and orgies are not me. But I am in Southern California now, I say, and there is no way I can *not* go to an orgy. . . ."

When the plane finally landed in L.A. it was four in the morning. I waited and let everyone file out ahead of me. Carl Ekern, my roommate, was among the last to leave. He put a friendly hand on my shoulder but he didn't tell me I would be all right. (Which is wise: how the hell does *any*body know?) Carl said, "Remember when we were watching the Miami-Minnesota game today on TV and we saw them carry that guy out with a hurt knee? Remember what you said? 'Shoot. Imagine. Last game of the season and he hurts his knee.' "

On crutches, I moved down the steps of the plane very carefully. United had a station wagon there to take me to the parking lot, where Steve Rosenbloom said he'd have his car waiting. He and Tut would take me to the hospital.

At the parking lot gate, Cindy and her dad were waiting. "Pat! Pat!" she cried, peering in at me. Steve stopped and told her to get in and let her dad follow us. She took my hand and kissed me and didn't ply me with a lot of questions. I told her what was happening. "All we can do," I said, "is wait and see. But I think I am through for the year."

December 12

By noon they had everything ready for the arthroscopy, including my leg, which they had given to some rookie to shave. He butchered me and it bled a lot. While I was waiting, I got phone calls from Andy Savitz in Boston and Joel Goldstein in St. Louis, my Rhodes colleagues, who were home for Christmas. They were worried about me—which pleased me. And then an attendant put me on a gurney and wheeled me into an operating room. Dr. Kerlan was there, along with Dr. Clarence Shields, and they told me to sign this little paper that gave them permission to operate on the knee if they found it necessary. "If we find extensive damage to either the hyaline cartilage or to the minisci," said Dr. Kerlan, "we'll have to remove it. If there's ligamental damage, we'll sew it up."

I don't know what kind of anesthesia they gave me, but they told me to count to a hundred—and then a sweet feeling overcame me and I didn't get past the number twelve.

I remember them sliding me off the gurney and back into my bed and then some time passed and in a very foggy state of mind I heard Cindy saying to me, "Pat, they didn't operate. Pat, they didn't have to operate. Pat . . ." And more time passed and when I woke up Cindy was still there smiling. I looked down and felt my knee under the sheet. I smiled, too, relieved they didn't have to go to the knife.

Neither Dr. Kerlan nor Dr. Shields was around. They'd left word that as soon as the anesthesia wore off, I could go home. I got there in time to see the fourth quarter of the Cowboy-Redskin game. Bill Kilmer and the Washington Redskins clinched a wild-card berth for themselves in the playoffs by beating the Dallas Cowboys in Washington 27–14. Maybe the Cowboys were a little laid back because they didn't *have* to win—and the Redskins did. But the stats were impressive: the Redskins netted 358 yards to the Cowboys' 203; and Kilmer completed 14 of 30 passes to Staubach's 5 for 22. And this after Bill Kilmer was picked up on charges of drunken driving in Maryland Friday night. Whatever he's drinking these days I'll have to order—for me and my generals.

December 13

NOW I AM IN THE HANDS OF GARY TUTHILL. HE'S GOT A complete rehabilitation program for me this week: I will have to leave the apartment at 6:15 A.M. for a session with Tut each morning and another one after practice in the evening. Today he packed my leg in ice, then applied an electro-galvanic stimulator to my knee, immersed in a whirlpool bath. These pulses contracted and expanded the muscles in the knee, just as exercising it would do—only faster. Then he took me over to an ultrasonic machine, applied a gel to my knee to keep the ultrasound waves from "burning," turned the wattage to one half and held the sonic applicator to my knee. "This," he said, "should help the muscle tone." Finally he taped the leg very firmly and said I ought to be ready to play.

Yesterday I didn't even give a thought to playing at Dallas. Today my knee doesn't hurt very much. Is it possible, I thought, that I can play? It is. Tut told me, "Pat, throw away those damn crutches. The docs says there's no extensive damage, just something they call a 'stretched ligature.' They say, 'If you feel like playing, then play.' So half your problem right now is mental." I looked searchingly at Tut. Hell, I'd played an entire game in high school with a broken shoulder. Was Tut now trying to tell me I was scared? He was.

"Sure," said Tut. "You were scared. Now you can put away your fears. You're going to be O.K."

By God, I said to myself, maybe Tut is right. Maybe my knee is better than I think it is. I may make it.

That alone will give me more than enough reason to celebrate tonight when I join Tom Mack and the others at Trani's Majestic Café in San Pedro. It is my party and I am picking up the tab for "my linemen."

Sitting in the training room while Tut worked over my knee, I found some interesting items in the *Times*: Don Klosterman told John Hall that he's finally found a company, heh heh, to insure our quarterbacks from now on: Lloyd's of Warsaw.

Also, Charlie Maher had an interview in the *Times* with William F. Buckley, Jr., in town promoting his new book, *Airborne*. Buckley says sports contests excite people today because life, for most of them, is so "inconclusive." By contrast, an athletic contest usually ends up with a winner and a loser. "That," he says, "satisfies the eschatological impulse." I don't think Bill has to give us a theology of football: making touchdowns has nothing to do with death, resurrection, immortality or judgment. But in a relativistic age when nothing ever seems resolved, it does seem like a damn nice luxury to be able to ask someone what the score is—and get an answer.

December 14

WHAT A SPREAD THE TRANI FAMILY PUT ON FOR US! WE HAD
about a dozen pizzas and beer, just to get ready for dinner,
and then Mama and Papa Trani and a lot of other Tranis
started bringing on the food and the wine: about four or five
different kinds of pasta and veal and chicken and steak and
peppers and mushrooms and eggplant and squash.

We took our time and enjoyed the Italian cuisine and the
wine, too. In fact, we got absolutely sloshed. For some reason,
the Tranis had invited my old high school principal, Msgr.
Thomas Kiefer, the guy who wouldn't marry me and Cindy
because he said I wasn't a practicing Catholic anymore. I
hadn't spoken to him since then, but here he was, not dressed
in his sacerdotals but casually, right in the middle of me and
my rowdy linemen. Oh well, I said to myself, if Monsignor
Kiefer can stand us, we can stand him. What the good, conservative Monsignor had to stand was some talk that was
bawdy in the extreme. Dennis Harrah, blond and baby-faced,
six five and 257 pounds, was narrating his adventures at a
Newport Beach bistro. "So these bleeping chicks are up on
the bleeping stage taking off their bleeping clothes. And I'm
up there, too, taking my bleeping clothes off. . . ."

As Doug France, six five and 260, got more and more
drilled his talk became more and more profane. "So I'm
bleeping telling you, no bleeping bleep of a bleep can bleeping
well bleep around with me like that. And he bleeping didn't
want to bleep bleep bleep . . ."

"Psst," Tom Mack reminded Doug. "That's a padre sitting
across the table here."

172

"Oh," said France. "I'm sorry." But that didn't change things any. France continued: "Well, bleep that bleep, I bleeping told him . . ." Tom jabbed him in the ribs, again. "Oh, hell," said Doug. He rose with his glass in one hand and his napkin in the other and addressed Monsignor Kiefer. "Father, I'm sorry. I can't sit here across from you. I'm going down to the other bleeping end of the table."

Toward the end of this fine feast the Tranis brought out a giant rum cake that was suitably decorated with my name and those of my offensive linemen. I cut huge slabs and loaded them down with ice cream and the Tranis brought us big mugs of coffee to put a capper on one of our finest pig-outs of the year.

Earlier today, Tuesday, I appeared in Tut's training room at seven in the morning, went through all the paces he thought I needed and fit right back into the schedule of team meetings and workouts just as if nothing had ever happened. Lee Bennett and Kenny Myer and Jack Faulkner gave our offense the dope on Dallas. We'd seen them in preseason and we knew their personnel: Lee Roy Jordan, now in his fourteenth menacing year with the Cowboys, and some other pretty fine defenders including a substitute named Thomas Henderson who was supposedly the fastest linebacker in the league; Too Tall Jones, Jethro Pugh, Larry Cole, and Harvey Martin up front; and two of the finest safety men in the business, Charlie Waters and Cliff Harris, both playing their seventh years for a coach, Tom Landry, who was and is one of the greatest defensive coaches the game has ever seen.

Landry has a few new curves to throw at us. On obvious passing downs he will put thirteen men on the field, then yank two off at the last moment so we won't have a chance to see whether they're using a nickel defense or what. Coach Knox explained on the blackboard what they were doing last week against Washington. "They hustle in two extra defensive backs," he said, "numbers twenty-five and forty-two. And two fast young linebackers, numbers fifty-four and fifty-six. You could go crazy trying to guess which ones will stay in there and which ones come running out. But there's a way to stop that nonsense completely. A hurry-up offense. We'll just run a play while they still have thirteen men out there and that'll be the end to that."

Before our 12:30 workout Shack sidled up to me quietly and wondered whether I wanted to "take the practice" today. It was considerate of him; he wanted no awkwardness out there on the field and did not want to treat the others to an Alphonse and Gaston act by their supposed on-the-field leader (whoever that would be, me or Shack). I told him I'd take it. But then, after I stepped under the center and threw just once, I knew I wasn't yet ready. My knee hurt. I told Shack he'd better take the practice. I spent my time behind the huddle, watching, throwing easily.

Larry Merchant is doing a big story for NBC on the L.A. quarterback situation and interviewed me after practice. He asks good questions and probed more deeply into my feelings on the matter than many others have done. This is a ticklish story that the local writers would rather stay away from. Maybe it takes a New Yorker to apply A. J. Liebling's *farther-franker law*: "The farther you are away from a situation, the franker you can be about it." Merchant asked me how I'd feel about Joe Namath coming to the Rams. Larry may have some kind of hidden agendum here: I think he's trying to help Joe get a job in L.A. Well, I'd be happy to see Joe here—if he wouldn't mind playing Earl Morrall to our Bob Griese—namely me!

December 15

THE LEAGUE ANNOUNCED YESTERDAY THAT SIX RAMS MADE the Pro Bowl game, scheduled for January 17 in Seattle. This is an all-star team that really means something to those who make it. It's not selected by the sportswriters or the fans (as some leagues do) but by the coaches themselves. So it's a real honor.

Our guys who made it are: Ron Jessie, Rich Saul and Larry McCutcheon from the offense; and Jack Youngblood, Butch Robertson and Monte Jackson from the defense. They should have taken our entire front four, including Olsen, Brooks * and Dryer. But I guess they'd like to spread the honors around as much as they can.

December 16

I THINK I'VE MADE IT. I DIDN'T TAKE THE PRACTICE YESTER-day; but that was defensive day. Today, offensive day, I took it. This was important. We're using a lot of different for-mations against Dallas, a slot formation, a tight end in mo-tion, other subtle wrinkles. And I have to be up on them. When I ran full speed in our dummy scrimmage, my knee felt absolutely O.K. My passing was just fine. In fact, I was passing better than I have all year. There's something in the air with us this week and I'm breathing it in just like the others are. A sense of confidence. A sense (heightened in

* Editor's note: Later, the league added Brooks to the Pro Bowl squad.

175

me) of exhilaration. I was dead. And now I am alive again.

There was an unusual intensity today. Everybody running at full speed and the coaches' voices cracked a little sharper than usual. Coach Knox says this was the best single practice the Rams have had in four years. The club has me listed officially a "doubtful" starter in Dallas. But after today's practice, I know I am the one. If that happens, I will dread reading the comments in L.A.'s black press, which is trying to make Harris' job a racial issue.

According to A. S. (Doc) Young, a columnist for the Los Angeles *Daily Sentinel,* Harris' demotion is further proof of the Establishment's "injustice." Young writes: "At base, this country was built on stealing, grabbing, killing, and human exploitation. Perhaps, then, it was stupid of us to believe that it could be any other way, even in professional sports."

I had not realized how much a James Harris' success meant to the black community in L.A. (or at least the black press) until someone showed me this column by Doc Young. Now I think I am beginning to understand. Young continues:

> . . . in the last quarter of the twentieth century, it would seem logical to believe, to hope, to expect that sports people, if no one else, would be better and more deeply committed than they are . . . to right vs. wrong, morality, human dignity, humanity, civil rights, religion, fairness.
>
> The Los Angeles Rams have knocked us flat on the bedrock of reality; the Rams have knocked the romanticism out of us, babe! Thirty years after Branch Rickey and Jackie Robinson reintegrated baseball, 30 years after the Dan Reeves-owned Rams reintegrated the National Football League, not one black athlete ranks unchallenged as the No. 1 quarterback on an NFL team.

The reason for this? I do not think the fact that Shack is black has had anything to do with it. But Doc Young does. And the ironic thing is that in crying "racism," Doc Young is open to charges of racism himself. As Young wrote:

176

When Pat Haden, the current white people's choice, plays, his mistakes are ignored or minimized while accomplishments are overblown. When the Rams lose under Harris, "it's all Harris' fault," and the whole truth is never told. When the Rams lose under Haden, you can bet that the loss will be charged to someone else's "break-down."

Pat Haden's Rhodes Scholarship has been scandalously overblown while all sorts of negative statements, hints and inferences have been made about James Harris' intelligence. Were Unitas, Namath, Tarkenton, Staubach Rhodes Scholars?

A book should be written about James Harris. Here's a great MAN who began paying his NFL dues in 1969; an intelligent man, a great athlete, a man of great character, a leader (yes, I said: A LEADER!), a WINNER . . . and yet, he was forced to earn his job every cussworded week. He never was SURE he had the No. 1 position sewed up. Unlike a Namath, Stabler, or Staubach, he couldn't throw four or five interceptions in a losing game and KNOW, not pray or hope, that he still was No. 1.

What should the Rams have done? Here's Doc Young's "solution":

If Carroll Rosenbloom had been properly committed to James Harris, he would NOT have signed Pat Haden because he would have KNOWN that Haden, being a white former USC star in a USC city, being a white Rhodes Scholar from USC, being a media favorite, could only pose a devastating problem, even if he never played a minute!

If Carroll Rosenbloom had been properly committed to James Harris, he would have given him, as it is given to all white quarterbacks, the right or privilege to LOSE!

On the Rams I don't think even a white QB has that "right" or "privilege." For Doc Young to say so makes him sound like the guys he's criticizing. But I do understand where he's coming from.

177

December 17

THEY HAD A KIND OF WELCOMING COMMITTEE FOR US HERE in Dallas, a couple dozen handsome men and women who told us how happy they were to have us, and a couple of TV crews who wanted some time with Coach Knox—and myself. When I was able to break loose, Klein, Scrib, Saul and I took off for a place the desk told us about, Carlos and Pepe's. The place was packed, about half of them good-looking women who seemed to be available. We found that a lot of the Rams were already there, grabbed Doug France (who was unchaperoned at the bar) and found a table for dinner. The management sent us over a couple of bottles of wine, compliments of the house, and we relaxed.

We all felt good about the week's practice. Nobody talked about the "Dallas jinx"—but I am sure that their beating us the last couple of years made everyone work harder. The intensity of each practice bordered on grimness. We practiced at game-speed, everything full-tilt, pass patterns, everything. The dummy team—which came out wearing sleeveless yellow shirts over their regular jerseys with numbers of the Dallas players on them—did a great job of showing me all the Dallas "defensive looks." And Rob Scribner and company did some convincing imitations of Roger Staubach et al. Myself, I spent more time on our game plan. Though I was at Blair Field from 7 A.M. to about 6 P.M. every day, I still took extra film home to study at night. When I wasn't answering phone calls.

December 18

LIGHT WORKOUT TODAY IN IRVING, TEXAS. I FEEL DAMN good. The coaches have us very well prepared. I feel no pressure. I like the idea of being three-point underdogs. I even like the Astroturf here.

Knox told the press I would be starting—while almost everyone, myself included, was predicting that it would be Shack. I am asking myself why. Coach Knox had an excuse to start Shack this week. And he didn't. All I can figure is: I *am* the number one quarterback. And I was practicing well this week. There's no reason, therefore, for Knox *not* to start me.

We saw the beginning of the Minnesota-Washington game on TV and the end of the Oakland-New England game. The Vikes got some early breaks, and the Redskins never had much of a chance. Vikes 35–20. On the other hand, the Patriots could have beaten the Raiders, and should have but for some questionable penalties, some that went against them at crucial times, some that should have gone against the Raiders and didn't. Playing with a broken nose (smashed in the third quarter by George Atkinson), Russ Francis, New England's great tight end, narrowly missed catching a pass on the Oakland 20. He didn't catch it because he was being held along his entire pass route. No penalty. Final score: 24–21, Raiders.

December 19

BEFORE THE GAME COACH KNOX SAID WE'D HAVE TO CON-trol the ball and put some points on the board. Defensively, we'd have to play our best game of the year. He added: "We're also going to have some luck. Most teams that win in the playoffs are blessed by some luck. But luck is a residue of design. If we hustle like hell, we'll make our own luck."

Well, we did all those things. But the guys who did them best were our defense. We came off the field winners, 14–12. And in the locker room as we pulled off our pads and tossed our jocks and T-shirts and socks in the middle of the floor, we chanted for ten minutes: DEE-FENSE! DEE-FENSE! DEE-FENSE! DEE-FENSE! It was the most emotional of all our victories, a hell of a football game against a very fine Dallas team. And we won. And we're going to Minnesota on Christmas eve for the NFC Championship Game. And there'll be no doubt about who'll be playing quarterback. I will.

Early on, Dallas had good field position. In the first quarter they started three drives from their 43, our 28 and our 44. But all they produced with those opportunities was one 44-yard field goal.

After that we stormed back. I completed my first pass, an 11-yarder to Harold Jackson—and my second and third as well: an 11-yard swing pass to John Cappelletti and a 42-yarder to Harold Jackson.

That put us on the Dallas 13. Clutch took it off right tackle for 4. John took it the other way for 5. On third and one, Kenny wig-wagged a play that few expected: a roll-out run to the left by the crippled Ram quarterback. I got great blocks, including ones by Clutch and John, and flew into the end zone standing up. Touchdown: 74 yards in ten plays. Demps made the conversion and we were ahead 7–3.

Midway through the second quarter, however, Randy Jackson got a bad snap from center; it bounced at his feet and he got the kick off only to see it blocked by Charlie Waters. That gave the Cowboys the spark they needed. Stymied up to now by Jack Youngblood, Merlin Olsen, Larry Brooks and Fred Dryer, Dallas proved it wasn't giving up. They drove on us and then Staubach hit Butch Johnson, a rookie from Cal Poly Pomona, for 18 yards down to our 2. On the Cowboys' third try from there, Scott Laidlaw finally plunged in for the TD. So Dallas had a 10–7 lead at halftime.

That didn't seem to matter to us. We all felt fine, that we could do anything we wanted. Maybe it was that Mass Father John Manion celebrated for us this morning. Or the inspirational service given by Bill Glass, once a great defensive tackle for the Cleveland Browns, at the other meeting. Or maybe just our own confidence in our own preparations. I felt fine. I'd run a bit and nothing hurt. I wouldn't let it hurt. I'd completed my first five passes. And our defense was giving Staubach more trouble than the Dallas defense was giving me. We felt that we could pass and run against the Cowboys. We believed that we'd stopped their run (they got only 45 yards in fifteen plays) and that they'd have to pass.

The third quarter turned out to be quite a duel between me and Staubach. On our first drive I passed four times for 51 yards and then I threw an interception to Benny Barnes on the Dallas 6. Staubach then came back and, on four completions, got 56 yards, only to be intercepted in turn by Butch Robertson on our 5.

We traded interceptions again. And then came another break for us, the kind of break Coach Knox had talked about earlier, the kind you make yourself: Staubach threw a screen pass to Preston Pearson. Freddie Dryer cracked him hard, he fumbled and Fred hugged it on the Dallas 39.

Did we smell the goal line then? We did. Clutch got 2 at right guard and 3 up the middle and on third and five, a passing down, when Dallas was juggling its thirteen men on the field, I called a quickie while they were still trying to get organized and run their two extra men off to the sideline. I made 6 on the play, a roll-out to the left, for a first down. Then, on a 34, over Tom Mack, John broke through what may have been a slightly demoralized defense for 16 big yards to the Dallas 12. They stiffened. Clutch, John and I ran for a total of 5 yards. Fourth and five. Better bring in Demps. He kicked the field goal to tie the game at 10–10.

But wait! A penalty on the play, a yellow flag on top of a pile of players around Tom Dempsey. Roughing the kicker. Should we take down the points and go for the TD? Hell, yes. We were in the fourth quarter now, and the way the game was going, we might not get this close to the Dallas goal again. Our offensive unit went back on the field. "Don't fumble!" cried Knox.

First and goal on the 3. I took it around left end for 2 yards. It seemed like I was running that play all afternoon, but it was a play the Dallas defense was daring me to call— and I was taking the dare. John hit the right side for no gain. Now what? Looking to the sideline, I told myself that Clutch should take it in. Good. The wig-wag said it *would* be Clutch on a 25 lead, between Dennis Harrah and John Williams and that's where Clutch took it, but young Thomas Henderson hurtled over the top and met Clutch at the line of scrimmage. It was a blow that might have put lesser men out of the game. Not Clutch. He kept his feet, bounced back and then nosed the ball into pay dirt. TD. Demps converted and it was Rams 14–Dallas 10.

That's the way the score remained until the two-minute

warning. Then disaster struck. With fourth and one on our 41 and a chance to put Dallas deep in its own territory, Rusty Jackson had another punt blocked—the same guy who did it the first time, Charlie Waters. The ball didn't go out of bounds until it got to our 17.

Over on our sideline Kenny Myer wailed, "I can't believe it!" But Coach Knox kept his cool. "They can't tie it with a field goal," he said. "They need a TD."

Ray Malavesi said, "They'll have to be good. They won't get anywhere running. I guarantee it."

Tom Landry didn't even try to run on first down, Staubach completed a pass to Butch Johnson in the end zone. Touchdown? No. Butch had one foot out of bounds. Two more passes went incomplete; we had perfect coverage. From the shotgun, however, on fourth and ten, Roger the Dodger was capable of anything. He faded. He threw—complete to Billy Joe Dupree 9 yards across the line of scrimmage. But he wasn't alone. Dave Elmendorf and Bill Simpson met him there and stopped him cold. One yard short.

We took over, first and ten on the 8-yard line, with one minute and a half to go. Three safe handoffs to John got a total of 5 yards. Still 34 seconds on the clock. But Dallas had no more time-outs. In went our punting team. Jackson went back in punt formation, into our end zone. He dawdled. And dawdled. The refs intervened and penalized us 5 yards for delay of game. Now there were only four seconds left. But we had to kick it. Would Charlie Waters block it again? No. We wouldn't give him any more chances. Rusty Jackson took the snap, a good one, and ran as fast he could for the right sideline, looked up to see no seconds on the clock, heard the gun and spiked the ball to the Astroturf. It was the first time any of us had ever seen anyone take a safety and spike the ball in the process.

But we'd won. We'd beaten one of the best teams in football, in the stats and, this time, on the scoreboard, too. And we were headed for Minnesota.

December 20

ACTUALLY, MY KNEE WAS A LITTLE SORE. PSYCHOLOGICALLY, however, I was in no mood to feel any pain. That's the difference between winning and losing. When you're winning, you can overlook a broken bone. When you're losing, you put yourself on the doubtful list with a sore toe.

We didn't even look at the Dallas film together. It was there if anybody wanted to see it. Most of us went out to run and the coaches got right to work preparing for Minnesota—in Minnesota, we're sorry to say. It will be my second Christmas in a row away from home.

December 21

DAY OFF TODAY. GAVE ME A CHANCE TO DO SOME CHRISTMAS shopping.

And then tonight Cindy and I went out and got a tree, brought it home and decorated it alone, together. This will be the extent of our Christmas celebration. When we beat Minnesota, I'll come home and celebrate Christmas—and New Year's—in a proper fashion.

December 22

THE COACHING STAFF GAVE US OUR BOOKS TODAY ON MIN-
nesota. It helps, of course, that we've already seen this team
once this year—except for the presence of Wide Receiver
Ahmad Rashad, whom the Vikes acquired from Coach Bud
Grant's old friend, Jack Patera of the Seahawks, in October.
Rashad, the former Bobby Moore of Oregon, is a game
breaker. And a real inspirational player as well.

Still and all, my book on the Vikes is fifty pages thick.
Coach Knox is not big on slogans. But on page one of this
tome are the reminders: "ATTACK! BE AGGRESSIVE!" And
another: "$$ BE READY TO PLAY YOUR BEST $$$."

A note to our linemen says: "Our big concern is the 5-man
line, which gives them a man-on-man pass rush with PAGE
running around most centers. Line stunts from this formation
are most evident. Lock them up, giving our QB time to throw
and you won't see it anymore."

Our scouts tell me that I won't have to fear too much dogging by the Viking linebackers. "They dog eleven percent of
the time," my book said. "Their dog percentage will go up
once they get behind. They dog most on second + 3-6 or
second + 1-2. Also: near either goal line. The Vikes are number one in the league versus the pass. They've had nineteen
interceptions this year. And 45 sacks. Watch out for Number
22, Krause. Look him off. Know where he is."

Our offensive strategy seems clear. We'll do better trying
to run on this Minnesota bunch. If we can. And, based on
how we (and the 49ers) did against them earlier in the
season, we know we can.

Defensively, we also know what to expect. The Vikes are a passing team. First in the league in passing, with 204 yards per game. They don't run to set up the pass. They pass to set up the run. Number 44, Chuck Foreman, can break loose at any time. He is also the best pass-catching back in the league. Sammie White, the Rookie of the Year, is no slouch either. He had fifty-one receptions this year, ten TD's, and an average of 17.8 yards per catch.

I got a look at Carl Ekern's book to see what our scouts say about Fran Tarkenton. He has a 61.9 percent pass completion average, has thrown for seventeen TD's. He's been sacked twenty-five times. But he's only thrown ten interceptions. The book went on: "He is a smart quarterback. Can read defenses well. Spends lots of time on film work, so he knows his opponent well. He likes sprints and roll-outs. Look for the 'bomb' after a big play by the opponent and change of possession. He likes to be cute, so you can expect action passes, especially out in the field on second and third down short yardage situations. He will fool you with his arm strength. Don't get careless. Plaster the receivers when he scrambles."

Mentally, I think we will be ready for them. There hasn't been a game this year when our coaches haven't had us absolutely well prepared. Emotionally, I do not know. But many of us were encouraged today when a fight broke out between Terry Nelson and Hacksaw Reynolds. The coaches just stood back and let them both go to it for a good long time before they broke it up. And when they did, the rest of us cheered. We're pros, but playing in the NFC Championship Game isn't just your average game; we need all the emotion we can muster for this one.

December 23

I DID NOT SLEEP WELL LAST NIGHT. THERE'S BEEN TOO MUCH hassle this week and I stayed up too late Monday and Tuesday nights so I thought I'd go to bed early. Along about 9:30 or so, however, the phone rang and Cindy found it was Jim Klobuchar, sports columnist of the Minneapolis *Star*. He had to talk to me. Cindy told him I was already asleep. He insisted. Now I was awake—and angry. What was so important? After a couple more minutes of palaver from Klobuchar I got up and grabbed the phone from Cindy.

What did Klobuchar want? Apparently nothing at all. He asked the same damn questions everybody had been asking me all week. And I gave him the same damn answers. I hung up, angry. And then I tossed and turned all night, thinking about what we could do to the Vikings' defense. Coach Knox had us put in a new play this week against the Minnesota goal line defense, a flanker reverse to Ron Jessie. We need something like that: that goal line defense of theirs is the best in the league—and we ought to know from experience. Against the Vikes, we are going to try something a little different on our pass blocking. The blockers are going to invite the rushers inside—so that I can slip outside occasionally and get a little more time to throw. We might be able to make some big plays that way. Of course, if this ploy backfires, they can make some big plays, too.

I guess I am not the only one thinking about big plays. I got a special delivery letter today from a guy in aerospace who describes himself as a "Sunday quarterback." In it he diagrams a pass play that has worked well for him in touch football games, "usually on the first play of the game or of the second half." It is called a "double receiver split." I wonder how many guys who watch the Rams every week have similar fantasies. Imagine: to send a play to the Rams' quarterback and then see him win with it in the NFC Championship Game! I am not knocking the fantasy. Multiplied many times over, it helps pay my salary.

December 24

MINNEAPOLIS. WHAT A CHRISTMAS EVE! IN A HOTEL AWAY from home, to play a football game in an icehouse. The temperature was 5 degrees above zero when we landed tonight and took our buses to the Registry Hotel. We didn't have to go out, as we usually do. The Rams gave us a Christmas Eve dinner in the hotel—to keep us together on a night when it would be too easy to go out and drink too much.

At dinner tonight I sat between Shack and Harold Jackson. Shack told stories about white-only drinking fountains in Louisiana and having to sit in the back of the bus. On Christmas Eve. Joy to the world. But Shack isn't just replaying old movies in his mind. Only last year he was stopped by a Los Angeles policeman, arrested, put in jail. For what? He was a passenger in a car being driven by his girlfriend. She had no driver's license, no registration. So the cop took *Shack* off to jail!

I talked, briefly, to Cindy tonight on the phone. She was at her parents' home in Hancock Park and I was more than a few thousand miles away. I am preoccupied with this game and, I am afraid, not a very loving husband.

December 25

GRAY, OVERCAST SKIES TODAY. MAYBE IT WILL SNOW. NO, someone says, it is too cold to snow. He is wrong. After our workout this morning in Metropolitan Stadium, that giant Erector set across the road, it did start snowing. Dandy. Somebody else said, "No, don't knock the snow. There's a tarp on the field. And as long as the cloud cover stays, it'll be comparatively warm, between twenty and thirty degrees. If a wind comes up and blows the clouds away, however, it'll go down to below zero. And if the wind keeps blowing, the chill factor will be minus ten or minus twenty degrees." A strange place to play for a national title.

At midday we had a Christmas Mass celebrated by Coach Knox's padre, Father John Manion of Seton Hall. Father Manion has been a good loyal chaplain. He tells me he was a "waterfront priest" for a long time in New Jersey. There, more than one man died in his arms. Good training for a chaplain in the NFL. Not too many Rams were at the Mass. But Carroll Rosenbloom was. I wonder if he prayed for a win here? I would if I were he; I'd take all the help I could get. The football isn't round and it takes funny and often fateful bounces.

I would also pray that their defensive back Nate Allen gets the flu or something. The league has a press book here on the game that includes thumbnail summaries of each Vikings' and Rams' game this year. In the Vikings' wrapups Nate Allen's name keeps popping up:

"Minnesota 10, Los Angeles 10— . . . Nate Allen

189

snuffed out Los Angeles' only scoring threat in overtime when he blocked a 20-yard Dempsey field goal try. . . .

"Minnesota 10, Detroit 9— At Pontiac Stadium, Nate Allen's block of a bobbled conversion attempt provided Minnesota's winning margin. . . .

"Minnesota 17, Pittsburgh 6— . . . Foreman scored in the second quarter after Nate Allen intercepted a Terry Bradshaw pass and Allen's fourth-period fumble recovery of a punt snap set up Foreman's four-yard TD burst. Allen had another interception and blocked a conversion attempt.

"Minnesota 24, New York Giants 7— . . . Following an opening field goal, Nate Allen returned a blocked punt 28 yards for a touchdown. . . ."

Tonight we had another Rams Christmas party, this time a turkey dinner and then a lot of gift giving. We had all drawn numbers last week, so that everyone would get one gift; tonight, we handed out the gifts—some of them too difficult for me to comprehend the meaning of. Bob Klein gave Rusty Jackson a set of children's blocks "from Charlie Waters" (Waters blocked two of Rusty's punts last week). Steve Preece gave Don Klosterman a dart board he made himself; on it was a picture of the entire squad under the headline "On The Trading Block, 1977." Rich Saul gave Hacksaw Reynolds a tin cup (for his pencils) and a pair of dark glasses. Jerry Wilcox gave Dr. Clarence Shields a butcher knife. Harold Jackson gave our equipment man, Don Hewitt, a T-shirt that read SIGN THE BALLS. Ron Jaworski gave Kenny Myer a kids' game called "Football Strategy." And Butch Robertson gave Ron Jaworski something he called a "Polish Salad"—which is indescribable.

As we left the party we noticed that in another large room of the hotel another big party was going on. It was a reception and buffet put on by Commissioner Pete Rozelle and the league for the members of the press. Nothing too fancy, I was told, but a good chance for the writers to meet one another and exchange their barbs. One thing I have noticed: when their teams get this far, there's no more objectivity left —the writers root unashamedly for their home teams. It's natural enough. If the Vikes go to the Super Bowl, a lot of writers will go to Pasadena. If the Vikes lose, they'll stay home.

And then there's Jim Klobuchar, the columnist for the Minneapolis *Star*. Now I find that he has collaborated with Fran Tarkenton on a current best-selling autobiography. If Tark goes to the Super Bowl, he has told one of our writers, he stands to make an extra forty thousand dollars. I'm sure Jim wasn't thinking of that when he got me out of bed Wednesday night to ask me inane questions and ruin my night's sleep. But if he wasn't, what *was* he thinking of?

Coach Knox had a press conference today after our workout and some of it made the TV news tonight. Chuck pointed out one fact about the Rams that makes him a little proud: "This is the only time in the history of the NFL," he said, "that a team has made the playoffs four consecutive years with four different starting quarterbacks. In 1973 it was John Hadl. 1974 James Harris. In 1975 Ron Jaworski. In 1976 Pat Haden."

What does this mean? It is a proof, I think, that this game of football is, above all, a coaching game. For Knox, it means that the quarterback's identity isn't the most important thing in getting to the playoffs, it's every other damn detail that he and his staff can think of, from the opening of training camp in July up to and including the last regular season game.

Still and all, I think Chuck would like to see a familiar face (mine!) out there when the Rams go to the playoffs again next year.

191

December 26

BLUE SKIES TODAY, A GOOD WIND, AND A CHILL FACTOR OF zero degrees Fahrenheit. Maybe this is why the smart money has made the Vikings 4½-point favorites.

Carroll Rosenbloom was in the locker room while we were getting suited up; he didn't look too optimistic. "Cheer up, boss," I said. "There's no doubt in my mind. We're gonna win this one." I was thinking to myself, our own preparation and self-confidence aside, that the temperature would be the same on both sides of the field.

Don Hewitt had come as prepared as anyone could be. He had long johns for the linemen and pantyhose for the backs and ends; they'd keep us warm, he said, but they wouldn't slow us up either. He also had jars of cream called Frost Guard, which we rubbed on our hands and feet. The legend on the label said it was designed to "Keep Out Cold."

The first quarter was ours statistically: we ran twenty-two plays to their five. We got seven first downs to their one. We outgained them 89 yards to 16. But the Vikes were ahead 7–0. The cold wasn't bothering us. But the funny bounces were.

Here's what happened: On our second possession we drove 54 yards in twelve plays and didn't score. On a play we'd put in for this game Jessie took the ball in for a TD on a flanker reverse from the Viking 4-yard line. But the refs didn't see it that way. They put the ball down on the 6-inch line and then, on third down, Coach Knox called for a quarterback sneak. I thought I made it in. Again the refs denied us the six points.

What now? I'd have tried for the TD. Knox sent in Tom Dempsey instead for the "automatic" field goal.

It wasn't quite automatic. Nate Allen broke through on our left side, blocked the kick and Defensive Back Bobby Bryant, swooping in from the other side, picked the ball up on a lucky bounce on the 10-yard line and sped unmolested for 90 yards and a Minnesota touchdown.

That didn't take any of the vinegar out of our attack. We came right back with another good drive. Clutch ran for 15 yards, slanting inside right end and cutting back to the left. He ran the same play inside left end for a gain of 10. I passed to Harold Jackson for 14 yards to the Vikings 21. There John Cappelletti fumbled; he did so while giving a good second effort; maybe the ball was stripped from his hands. On this cold day that was not a difficult thing to do.

But things were getting out of hand. Minutes later Rusty Jackson dropped a center snap and had a punt blocked on our 8. They got zilch on three downs; but they did kick a field goal. They'd gotten a ten-point lead on us in September. Now they had one again. It didn't faze me. In fact, I came right back with a bomb to Ron Jessie down the right sideline; he was in the clear and should have had a TD. But the Vikings' Jeff Wright, badly beaten, did the only thing he could: he plowed right into Jessie, illegally on two counts: 1) face-guarding and 2) hitting Jessie before the ball arrived. Penalty? Nope. Bob Klein, the closest Ram to the ball, protested. But no one else in the stadium did and we were just out of luck. With six seconds to go in the half I hit Jessie with another bomb; but he was pushed out of bounds as he caught it and we ran out of time.

There was no ranting or raving during the intermission, no panic. We knew we were a superior ballclub and that it was just a matter of time before we got untracked. There were no major adjustments to make on offense. Nor on defense either. We were making yards ourselves. And the Vikes were making few. Tark had 52 yards passing; Foreman, McClanahan and Robert Miller had 37 yards rushing.

On one play early in the third quarter, however, Foreman broke a tackle at the line of scrimmage, then juked Bill Simpson, who was coming in on him for the kill, and rambled 62 yards to our 2-yard line. Another Viking touchdown, mainly on one big play. Now it was 17–0. An impossible situation, especially for a rookie quarterback in a playoff game.

I didn't even think about that. I just came out throwing. And got nowhere. I was off the mark on my first pass deep down the middle to Harold Jackson. I got sacked on my second by Carl Eller. I threw my third into the dirt. Over on the sidelines Coach Knox told Shack to warm up, but he sent me back in when Monte Jackson got us the ball with an interception in the end zone. This would be my last chance to put some points on the board. I did, leading the offense on an 80-yard drive in six plays to our first touchdown. Scrambling a lot, I passed for almost 60 yards, Clutch ran for 22, including a 10-yard ramble over two tacklers for the TD. Shack stopped warming up. Only trouble was: Tom Dempsey was wide on his point-after-TD: 17–6.

And then our two brilliant defensive ends, Fred Dryer and Jack Youngblood, got us the ball again deep in Viking territory. Freddie forced Tark to fumble; Jack picked it up and ran to their 8. Clutch bulled his way for 5 yards. Then I threw a lob deep in the end zone and Harold grabbed it. Demps made the conversion this time: 17–13. We were back in the ball game. The way we were playing, we knew we could do it. And we had a full quarter to do it in.

Somehow, we didn't. In retrospect I think we tried to pass too much. We'd caught up passing. But now we didn't have to hurry. We could run on these guys. We'd proved that. So why were we passing? Possibly because we were behind by four, not three. We needed a touchdown. Possibly because Minnesota's linebackers Hilgenberg, Siemon and Blair started playing rather more inspired ball and were holding Clutch and John to less than 5 yards on our first down situations. But the fact is that three successive drives ended when I could not find receivers open on third and long.

We got another chance. With lots of time left, three minutes and fifty-five seconds, we started another drive from our 37. I connected on a couple of passes and John ran once for 11 yards. First and ten on the Viking 39. We still could have run. But no: the coaches sent in three straight passes— all went incomplete. The Vikes weren't leading the league in pass defense for nothing. They had good coverage.

Fourth and ten on the 39 with two minutes and forty seconds to go. We could have punted. We could have gone for the first down. Instead, at the sideline, Coaches Knox and Myer and I figured we'd go for broke right here. They'll be playing for a short pass, Myer said, you should find Jessie or Jackson clear on a sixty-five pass. I did. I faded to pass, reading their free safety, Paul Krause. He went weak side, so I looked the other way, for Jessie, who blew right by Nate Wright in the clear. I had no time to look at Harold and I threw one of my better passes of the day to Ron. This was it. I could see the points on the board: 19–17. Maybe 20–17.

But then a purple shirt came flying across the field. Number 20, and he went high into the air on our 8-yard line to take the ball away from Jessie, who didn't even see him coming. Who the hell was that? And where did he come from? It was Bobby Bryant, their right cornerback, who should have been with Jackson. Well, it was a super play, that's all I can say. I guess I should have given a look to Harold; when Bryant saw me concentrating on Jessie, he took a chance, a chance that paid off—big.

Because I never saw the ball again. Tark, almost sacked,

got off a little dink pass to Chuck Foreman over the middle; he rambled with it for 57 yards to our 12-yard line (and came out of the game on the play after a clean tackle by Monte Jackson). The final indignity came, however, when with only seconds remaining, Foreman's sub, Sammy Johnson, ran 12 yards for a Viking touchdown. Final score: Vikings 24—Rams 13.

We trooped into the dressing room a despondent bunch, grabbing Cokes and heading for our locker stalls, throwing our helmets down and ripping off our shoulder pads and pants while we waited for everyone to get in. As I was sitting there I couldn't help but notice the spotlights over a small plywood stage in the middle of the dressing room and two television cameras and a tangle of cables along the floor. CBS had been ready. But we lost. And no one was there, no cameramen, no commentators, just the silent cameras. Tom Brookshier, I imagined, was over in the other dressing room where the Vikes were even now opening their champagne. I took a sip of my Coke and listened to Knox. "Don't let the writers in for a while," he said. He was near tears. "I'm proud of you all," he said. "You came back today, you came back big. You got nothing to be ashamed of."

C.R. came by, talking to many of us privately. I told him I was sorry. "It wasn't your fault, kid," he said. "It's just a shame to see a game dominated by the officials and taken away by such bad calls. Jessie was in there on that reverse. And that made all the difference. We had a TD. Then, on the next play, they got a TD on a lucky bounce. That's a fourteen-point difference."

Then the press trooped in, not the national press or the local press, but our own L.A. press, the guys who had followed us all season: Florence, Krikorian, Chortkoff, Roberts, Cox, Murphy, Joe Hendrickson of the Pasadena *Star-News*. "They're a good football team," I said. "They came up with a lot more big plays than we did. Bryant made some big plays. I should have made more of them myself. That's the quarterback's job." I picked at a run in my black pantyhose. "The cold? It wasn't a factor. It may have looked like it, the way I threw the ball sometimes."

Rich Roberts of the Long Beach *Press-Telegram* commiserated with me. Gently, I cut him off. "Listen," I said. "This is just my first year. I am mostly disappointed for Merlin Olsen. I have so much admiration for this human being. Ahh, well. Both his life and mine will go on."

Bob Cox of the South Bay *Breeze* asked me if I would have gone for a field goal from the 6-inch line. I said, "That's not for me to say. That's the coach's decision. It's his ballclub. But if I'd done a better job on my quarterback sneak the play before, we wouldn't have even had to make that decision."

And then I moved off to get a shower, past Hack Reynolds and Jack Youngblood and Merlin Olsen, who were trying to explain their views to the reporters, too. I heard one reporter ask Carroll Rosenbloom about a rumor that Knox was leaving the Rams. "What?" said Carroll. "No! Not on your life. Chuck. Chuck. This guy just asked me if you were leaving us and I told him I'd break your legs if you did. Right? Tell him, Chuck."

Chuck gave a tired smile. "That's right," he said. What's right? That Chuck's going to leave and that C.R.'s going to have his legs broken? Or what? I do not know.

On the bus leaving Metropolitan Stadium for the airport Bob Klein and I replayed much of the game. I said I should have called audibles on two different occasions, but didn't because I had already started my count and feared a penalty for delay of the game. "But I *should* have checked signals," I said with some force, "and begun again. Each of them could have been big plays, touchdowns."

Klein laughed. "Hell, Pat," he said, "every one of us can

talk about the plays that might have been. You can't criticize yourself for *not* calling a play. Talk about the plays you did call this year, the touchdown passes that got us this far!"

He was right, I guess. But I couldn't help thinking what might have been. Then I stopped for a moment and listened to a cluster of defensemen across the aisle. Jack Youngblood, Hack Reynolds, Fred Dryer and Butch Robertson were replaying the game, too; and, although we had lost the game, their voices came across as joyful and eager and it was easy for me to see that these were guys who played football because it pleased them to play—win or lose. They did the best they could. No one did any better. But winning—or losing— a crazy game like this one was something that was not, ultimately, under their control. There'd always be another year. And when there wouldn't be another, well, then, it was a good career. What's next? That, I guess, was the only way to go.

Carroll Rosenbloom caught me as I was getting on the plane. "What happened," he said, "on that last pass to Jessie?"

I told him what I had told the press: I should have looked Bryant off before I hit Jessie. But I didn't have the time. They held Ron up at the line of scrimmage and it was either get rid of it right away or get sacked. C.R. nodded.

Maybe somebody will tell C.R. that I should have thrown the ball later on a lower trajectory. And maybe somebody else will point out that I could have thrown the ball sooner on a higher trajectory. But I threw a very good pass; and it happens that it was, under the circumstances, the only pass I could have thrown.

To C.R. my pass was only incidental. We lost the game, he went up and down the plane saying, because "the officials didn't have guts enough to call [Jessie's run] a TD." I don't know *why* they didn't call a touchdown. But I do know I saw Ron fall over the goal.

Through the plane, after takeoff, some of the younger men

198

were still replaying the thing. "Hey, Kenny," shouted Dennis Harrah, "you look at those movies and if I was holding on that play, you send me a bleeping telegram or call me a bleepbleeper, whatever you want, if I was holding." But the vets were letting it go.

The cowboys were playing country and western music, drinking Coors and talking about bulldogging steers. You could hear Jack Youngblood's robust voice all over the plane: "So this Black Angus steer come right over the top of me. . . . He's still going. They took seven stitches over each of my eyes."

Phil Boomgard, our United pilot, had the Pittsburgh-Oakland game on the airplane intercom if you wanted to turn to Channel 4. Somebody with a headset said Oakland was killing Pittsburgh; Harris and Bleier weren't playing. "Shoot," said somebody, "Oakland? We can beat Oakland!"

December 27

CRITICS' CORNER. NATURALLY, JIM MURRAY WROTE HIS humdinger of the year this morning in the *Times*.

> Bloomington, Minn.—You don't start a poker game by throwing away a pair of aces in the hopes of hooking dueces and treys.
> You don't start a golf tournament on a par-5 hole and pull out a nice safe 7-iron on the tee.
> You don't bunt with the bases loaded and two men out.
> You don't step back when you get the other guy on the ropes.
> And you don't start championship football games by going for a field goal from the 6-inch line of the other team.
> The Rams won't be in the Super Bowl again this year because that's precisely what they did.

They put the Minnesota Vikings in the Super Bowl—which they'll have to answer for—because they lacked the killer instinct. It was like Dempsey going to the jab after he had just floored his man, Ruth choking up, Jerry West passing off under the basket . . .

There is a thing in football called "The Book." The way football coaches treat it, you'd think it was found in the Dead Sea or graven in stone and given to Moses on Mt. Sinai or it's a testament compiled by Matthew, Mark, Luke and John.

The "Book" says that when you drive down to the 6-inch line, you put some points on the board. And the Rams did. They put 7 on the board for Minnesota. . . .

Yeah, in retrospect on a Monday morning, Jim was right. But he wouldn't have been if we'd been held again on the 6-inch line—and lost the game by the margin of a field goal.

December 28

CRITICS' CORNER. MAYBE THE BEST COMMENT ON THE GAME came today from the *Herald-Examiner*'s racetrack writer, Gordon Jones.

Jones writes that football officials should follow the example of racing stewards, who use "instant replays and alternate camera angles to check and recheck dozens of incidents every race." He continues: "If the NFL even roughly matched modern-day horse racing's built-in protection system for gladiators and spectators alike it would have been Los Angeles 7, Minnesota 0. . . . And Oakland's Raiders would have themselves a real football game on January 9."

Chuck Barnes phoned today with good news. He's persuaded ABC to let me do the color commentary on the Hula Bowl in Hawaii January 8. I played in the Hula Bowl myself and the game is probably the best of the postseason all-star games. There'll be some Trojans in the game: Ricky Bell, Vince Evans and Shelton Diggs. And some Trojans *on* the game, too: in addition to myself, ABC is hiring Lynn Swann to do sideline interviews. Keith Jackson, one of ABC's best, will do the play-by-play. Chuck didn't tell me how much ABC will pay. But that isn't important to me. It's the exposure. There's a potentially lucrative sideline for me in commercials and endorsements.

And NBC wants me and some of the other Rams to come over to Burbank for the taping of a show called "The Mad Mad Mad Mad World of the Superbowl." It'll be a series of sketches built around the football theme, quick little bits along the lines of the old "Laugh-In" program, "hosted" by a well-known quarterback named Joe Namath and two actresses who play in "Charlie's Angels." From the Rams, NBC would like to have me, Ron Jessie, Jack Youngblood, Larry McCutcheon and John Cappelletti. At $500 each.

December 29

I SAW CARROLL ROSENBLOOM TODAY UP AT HIS BEL AIR mansion. The man is amazing. He's forgotten all about this season. He's making plans for next year and he would like me to know I figure in them. There's only one thing: he wants me to keep working with weights, strengthening my arm.

At home the phone doesn't stop ringing. Tonight a pair of agents, Mark Zavit and Mike Merko, were on the horn, talking about all the commercials and personal appearances I could be making in the next few months. They said I could make $80,000 on commercials alone.

All this sounds good, but it's all so fleeting. I might make $80,000 on commercials in 1977, but ten years from now I might make nothing—or be a marginal celebrity with occasional shots on "Hollywood Squares."

Not for me. It's too easy now and it could turn my head away from a career in law. I don't need the money. I grossed $73,000 this year. Cindy and I were able to put a $20,000 down payment on a condominium in Newport Beach and we've got $20,000 in the bank besides. That's enough.

January 1, 1977

THE ROSE BOWL GAME. I WATCHED ON THE TUBE AS MY alma mater, USC, beat a Michigan team that some writers had said was one of the greatest college teams of all time. Score: 14–6. And my understudy at Troy, Vince Evans, did better than all right, completing fourteen out of twenty passes for 181 yards. What I liked the most was his perfect fake to Charles White, hurdling over the goal line, and then Vince's scamper around the left side for the go-ahead touchdown. It was a beautiful play—because it worked. Now if it hadn't . . .

January 2

SOMEBODY FROM *Time* PHONED ME TODAY WONDERING IF I could talk to some executives in town for the Super Bowl. They want to pay me five hundred dollars to have dinner with them and their wives at the Bistro in Beverly Hills on Friday night. I had to turn them down because I'll be in Hawaii then getting ready to cover the Hula Bowl for ABC.

January 3

MY BUSINESS MANAGER TOLD ME TODAY I OWED ANOTHER $9,000 in income taxes. I was under the impression that the Rams were withholding all my taxes, but he said they didn't withhold enough. It seems that I am in the 50 percent federal tax bracket and I pay 11 percent to the state of California. That means that I'll be earning about $28,000 this year, not $73,000. "That'll teach you to vote Democratic," said John McKay when I told him what was happening to me. But hell, the state and federal governments have both been run by Republicans for most of the past decade. This isn't Republicans or Democrats. It's just the way the world is changing.

January 4

TODAY I HAD TO GO DOWN AND GET MY PICTURE TAKEN WITH the poster child for the Crippled Children's Fund, a beautiful little guy named George Vick who would probably never take a fluid step in his life. And that put things back into perspective for me.

Yesterday I was bitching because I was only earning thirty-nine cents on the dollar and today I am counting my blessings:

203

I have a good mind, two arms and two legs and a woman who loves me. What more do I really need?

Then I went to Coach Knox's offices in Long Beach to talk with him about the quarterback situation. There's a possibility Shack will be traded, and Ron has made it clear by his words and his actions that he no longer wants to be a Ram. Now what? The Rams need another quarterback, maybe two more. But who? Coach Knox was talking about getting Joe Namath or maybe Dan Pastorini, who's unhappy at Houston, and then the phone rang. It was Carroll Rosenbloom, who knew that I was having this session with the coach.

C.R. had just seen a piece by Dave Anderson of *The New York Times,* running this afternoon in the *Herald-Examiner.* It was an article openly advocating Namath's move to L.A. and C.R. told Knox to tell me that the Rams weren't buying any of it. "Tell Pat not to worry about Namath," C.R. said.

I was pleased that C.R. would take the trouble to call. He is concerned about my feelings. This bodes well for next year when we will need at least one more quarterback. It seems to me that the Rams can: 1) get a journeyman quarterback like John Hadl or Craig Morton or Billy Kilmer to back me up or 2) go after a blue-chip quarterback like Dan Pastorini —in which case we will have a brand new quarterback controversy next fall. Naturally, I hope the Rams decide on alternative number one.

After I finished with Knox I went out and bought a paper and read Anderson. It was an incredible piece of advocacy journalism, full of specious reasoning on why the Rams needed Namath. "When a team has three quarterbacks, it usually has none," wrote Anderson, ignoring the fact that neither Ron nor I would have seen much action at all if Shack hadn't been hurt—twice. And that, once I'd gotten the starting job, neither of the others was able to take it away from me—even though they were both better quarterbacks last year than Namath was.

Anderson didn't say how Namath could help the Rams. He seemed more interested in explaining how the Rams could help Joe: 1) With the Rams, Joe might make it to the Super Bowl. 2) Namath has already played under Coaches Knox and Myer when they were both assistants on the Jets. That would make the transition easier for Joe. 3) Playing for the Rams would provide a rebirth for Joe "after seven seasons in the Jets dungeon." And "Namath needs a reason to care about winning again." 4) "Namath's ego needs to be stimulated. Namath doesn't belong in Denver or Houston or New Orleans; he belongs in New York or Los Angeles where the scene suits his style . . . Beverly Hills Joe."

Anderson seriously suggested that Namath would even take a cut in salary if he could exchange Broadway for Sunset Boulevard. He gets $500,000 a year from the Jets. With the Rams, he'd "settle" for a $150,000 salary, a $50,000 bonus if the Rams win their first playoff game, a $100,000 bonus if they win their second and a $200,000 bonus if they win the Super Bowl, this for a guy who was the fourteenth-rated passer this year in the AFC.

January 5

SHACK PHONED ME TODAY TO DISCUSS RON JAWORSKI'S appearance this week on Hank Konysky's "Sportstalk" over KABC Radio. I'd heard from others that Ron was taking some cheap shots at me on the air—saying that being a Rhodes scholar didn't necessarily make me an NFL quarterback and that I didn't have an NFL arm. Shack said that Ron had no business saying these things. But that when Ron had teed off on the Rams organization, he, Shack, had to say right on, they were true. "These guys run this thing like a business," said Shack, "and if you don't produce . . ." His voice trailed off and I agreed with him, pro football is a business. He said, "That means that the same thing that happened to me is going to happen to you. You're popular around here, you had a good season but you better get to the Super Bowl in the next couple of years or you're going to be gone."

Well, yes. I had to say Shack was right. Unwittingly, of course, he was giving testimony against those who theorized that Shack didn't make it in L.A. because he was black. If Shack had taken us to the Super Bowl, he could have been purple with yellow polka dots. C.R. doesn't care what color you are. The only question he asks is can you win?

However, going to the Super Bowl shouldn't be the only criterion with C.R.—and I don't think it is. Hell, *I* could have taken the Rams to the Super Bowl this year, my rookie season, except for one unlucky bounce of the ball at Minnesota!

A lot of fine quarterbacks have never taken their teams to the Super Bowl. But that didn't lessen their worth as premier players. So many things are beyond the control of the quarterback. One man jumping offside in a crucial situation, one fumble inside the five, one guy letting a man block a kick . . . I demand a lot of myself. But this is a game played by forty-three men. Next year, I don't know. Are things going to go my way or not? Will I have the breaks or not? Who knows?

There is only one way to avoid being a victim of the breaks, and that's to win every game by two or three touchdowns. Then the breaks don't kill you. But that's unrealistic: hey, the Vikings got to the Super Bowl this year by beating Detroit 10–9, Chicago 20–19, Seattle 27–21, Green Bay 17–10. And even now, though they are in the Super Bowl (something that eluded twenty-six other teams in the league) they still run the risk of being labeled "winners" or "losers" on the outcome of this one game.

January 6

HAWAII. KAHALA HILTON HOTEL. CHUCK AND I HAD A DRINK with ABC's Keith Jackson this afternoon and it was clear that Keith wasn't at all happy over ABC's decision to have me do the color commentary here at the Hula Bowl. He didn't have anything against me personally. He just didn't like the idea of athletes moving from the field to the broadcasting booth with such all-fired ease. He read me a lesson on what it takes to be a good announcer. I got the impression Keith would prefer if I started announcing high school sports in San Luis Obispo, instead of starting here at the top. What was I to say? All other things being equal, I'd rather have the national audience, the one thousand dollars plus expenses, the first-class jet travel, the limousine at the airport—and a few days in Hawaii. Not that I have anything against San Luis Obispo.
. . .

January 8

I SPENT SOME TIME TODAY AT BOTH THE EAST AND THE WEST camps, getting to know the players and familiarizing myself with the system of each coach, Johnny Majors of the East and

Mike White of the West. The ABC cameras will be allowed to kibbitz on sideline conferences and if I know what the numbers mean I can provide the viewers with some guidance about what's coming up. Experts aren't only supposed to know what has happened but also what is going to happen. We're all supposed to be futurists, I guess.

Rick LaCivita is a producer here for ABC. I met him at the Winter Olympics in Innsbruck and I find it's a pleasure to renew acquaintance. He's only twenty-four but a real ambitious guy who spends less than a month each year at home in New York.

It took me a while to get warmed up on the telecast. Keith Jackson told me he'd cue me, but he didn't, and I let some opportunities pass me by. Pretty soon, however, I was zinging right in there with my comments on the play. By the second half I was doing a passable job and ended up enjoying the entire experience. As far as All-Star games go, the Hula Bowl is one of the best—for the players and for the die-hard football fans who are still watching football this late in the season. Since the team that's ahead always kicks off here, the games tend to stay close, and this one was no exception.

That's why it was shortsighted of the game's directors to circulate ballots for the game's outstanding player very early in the third quarter. At that time most of the writers in the press box voted for Tony Dorsett, who hadn't done all that well except for one 47-yard run, but whose team was then ahead. In the fourth quarter, however, who emerged as the game's real hero? None other than my guy from SC, Vince Evans, whose scrambling and passing led the West to a 20–17 victory. After that, the announcement of Dorsett as the game's outstanding player sounded a little lame.

Chuck and I rode to the airport in an ABC limousine with Keith Jackson. "You think you want to make this a career?" asked Keith.

"Nope," I said. Sportscasting was fun, but hardly important enough to justify itself as a full-time occupation. What kind of life was it, anyway? Rick LaCivita spends three weeks a year at home and works under all kinds of pressure. I don't imagine Keith Jackson has much more time than that to devote to his family. Television sports may look glamorous, but it can't be that fulfilling.

January 10

RATHER THAN GO TO THE SUPER BOWL, CINDY AND I DECIDED to have a party at our apartment—as, I guess did many of the 76 million who watched the game on TV. John and Kim McKay came and a gang of our SC buddies, their wives and/ or girlfriends. We had about twenty, including Phil and Joe Boskovich, Joe Collins, Grek Brakovich (who is being trans-ferred to Delaware) and John Nelson.

We drank a lot and hooted and hollered (most of us) for the Vikings, but it wasn't their day. The ball didn't bounce quite as conveniently for them yesterday as it did two weeks ago against us. Early in the game, with the score still 0–0, the Vikes blocked yet another kick (their sixteenth of the season) and Bobby Bryant was in position to pick it up and take it in for a score (as he did against us). This time, however, the ball bounced high over his head and the Vikes had to settle for possession on the 5 instead of a TD. And then, they didn't get the TD. Brent McClanahan fumbled on second down, the Raiders took over and drove almost the length of the field to score. It was the fourth quarter before the Vikes put points on the board—after the Raiders had scored nineteen. And then it was too late. They say Tarkenton had a bad game.

But it is hard to play a good one when you have to throw on every down. And as soon as Oakland got ten points ahead, that's exactly what Tark had to do.

Against the Rams, I don't think Oakland would have gotten ten points ahead. And I also think we'd have moved the ball better than the Vikings did. Maybe we wouldn't have beaten Oakland. But we would have given them a helluva better game. That's the sad p.s. to our season.

But life goes on. After the game all twenty of us went out to dinner at Antonio's for Mexican food. Lots of tequila and lots of toasting, ending with a tipsy sendoff at the airport for John and Kim McKay, heading back to Tampa (where John's doing front-office work for the club and Kim's finishing school).

Amid all the nonsense said and written this week about the Super Bowl, Coach John Madden of the Oakland Raiders said there were two things that attract him to the game of football—the thrill of competition and being part of a team. "You're part of a group that's bigger than you," said Madden, "and you're in it with people who think it's as important as you do. You're seeking to achieve as a unit, and that's a very civilized thing to attempt, very human."

I couldn't agree more.

In a couple of days I will be going back to Oxford. I am sure that some there will ask me what my season with the Rams has "contributed." I do not know what I will tell them. I'm sure I'll think of something. (I could tell them I contributed $54,000 in taxes—but I won't.)

I do know that I have learned a great deal. I learned much more than how to read a red dog or a safety blitz or call an audible. There are certain things people learn just by being human, by talking with others, by listening, by feeling. I tried to do this with the Rams, a group of fine athletes, but very good and very interesting human beings as well. The irrepres-

210

sible Ron Jaworski, the ever-confident Butch Robertson, the idiosyncratic Jack Reynolds, the unloquacious Cullen Bryant; being around them was an education I couldn't get at Oxford, or anywhere else.

As diverse as the Rams were, from different parts of the country, different backgrounds, with different prejudices, biases and aspirations, we lived together, worked and ate together, won and lost football games and learned a lot together. I think we are better men for what we learned.

More than from any other, I learned from James Harris, a good man. He had every reason to dislike me and all that I stood for, but when I came into the picture he didn't bitch and make a scene, he helped me. He taught me the meaning of sacrifice for a team goal—despite every temptation to do otherwise. I can never thank him enough.

April 1

A COUPLE OF WEEKS AGO I HEARD THE RAMS HAD TRADED THE rights for Ron Jaworski's services to the Philadelphia Eagles. A week ago I got a reliable report that the Rams were sifting through some offers for James Harris. So it was no surprise today when I discovered that the Rams are now negotiating a contract with Joe Namath—who was just given free agent status by the New York Jets.

Obviously, the Rams need at least two quarterbacks, maybe three. And among those few proven veterans available to the Rams, I think I'd rather have Joe Namath around than almost anyone else. I'll still see a lot of action. And I can learn more than a little from Namath about football.

Of course, I can do something for him, too. I can introduce him to a few people in Hollywood . . .

APPENDIX

RAMS' ROSTER, 1976

NO.	NAME	POS.	HT	WT	AGE	EXP	COLLEGE
45	Bertelsen, Jim	RB-KR	5-11	205	26	5	Texas
90	Brooks, Larry	DT	6-3	255	26	5	Va. State-Petersburg
32	Bryant, Cullen	RB-KR	6-1	235	25	4	Colorado
22	Cappelletti, John	RB	6-1	217	24	3	Penn State
10	Dempsey, Tom	K	6-1	260	29	8	Palomar J.C.
89	Dryer, Fred	DE	6-6	240	30	8	San Diego State
55	Ekern, Carl	LB	6-3	220	22	R	San Jose State
42	Elmendorf, Dave	S-KR	6-1	195	27	6	Texas
79	Fanning, Mike	DT	6-6	260	23	2	Notre Dame
77	France, Doug	T	6-5	260	23	2	Ohio State
87	Geredine, Tom	WR-KR	6-2	189	26	3	Northeast Missouri State
11	Haden, Pat	QB	5-11	182	23	R	Southern California
60	Harrah, Dennis	G	6-5	257	23	2	Miami, Fla.
12	Harris, James	QB	6-4	210	29	7	Grambling
63	Horton, Greg	G	6-4	245	25	1	Colorado
29	Jackson, Harold	WR	5-10	175	30	9	Jackson State
28	Jackson, Monte	CB	5-11	189	23	2	San Diego State
9	Jackson, Rusty	P	6-2	190	26	R	Louisiana State
16	Jaworski, Ron	QB	6-2	185	25	3	Youngstown State
81	Jessie, Ron	WR	6-0	185	28	6	Kansas
76	Jones, Cody	DT	6-5	240	25	3	San Jose State
80	Klein, Bob	TE	6-5	235	28	8	Southern California
65	Mack, Tom	G	6-3	250	33	11	Michigan
30	McCutcheon, Lawrence	RB	6-1	205	26	4	Colorado State
50	McLain, Kevin	LB	6-2	238	22	R	Colorado State
83	Nelson, Terry	TE	6-2	230	25	3	Arkansas AM&N
74	Olsen, Merlin	DT	6-5	270	36	15	Utah State
49	Perry, Rod	CB	5-9	170	23	2	Colorado
39	Phillips, Rod	RB	6-0	220	23	2	Jackson State
20	Preece, Steve	S	6-1	195	29	8	Oregon State
54	Reece, Geoff	C	6-4	247	24	R	Washington State
64	Reynolds, Jack	LB	6-1	232	28	7	Tennessee
58	Robertson, Isiah	LB	6-3	225	27	6	Southern U.
57	Rogers, Mel	LB	6-2	230	29	4	Florida A&M
61	Saul, Rich	C	6-3	250	28	7	Michigan State
86	Scales, Dwight	WR-KR	6-2	170	23	R	Grambling
33	Scribner, Rob	RB-KR	6-0	200	25	4	UCLA
48	Simpson, Bill	S	6-1	180	24	3	Michigan State
78	Slater, Jackie	T	6-4	252	22	R	Jackson State
27	Thomas, Pat	CB	5-9	180	22	R	Texas A&M
75	Williams, John	T	6-3	256	31	9	Minnesota
85	Youngblood, Jack	DE	6-4	255	26	6	Florida
53	Youngblood, Jim	LB	6-3	239	26	4	Tennessee Tech

R — A first year player who has not previously been in an NFL training camp.

RAMS COACHING STAFF

Chuck Knox	Head Coach
Leeman Bennett	Receivers
Tom Catlin	Linebackers
Jack Faulkner	Special Assistant
Ray Malavasi	Defensive Coordinator
Ken Meyer	Offensive Coordinator
Elijah Pitts	Offensive Backfield & Special Teams
Ray Prochaska	Offensive Line
Jim Wagstaff	Defensive Backfield

RAMS' OFFENSE

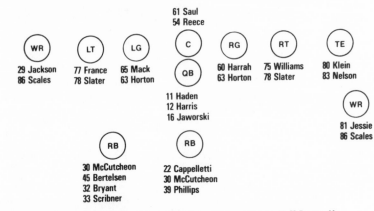

61 Saul
54 Reece

WR — 29 Jackson / 86 Scales

LT — 77 France / 78 Slater

LG — 65 Mack / 63 Horton

C

QB — 11 Haden / 12 Harris / 16 Jaworski

RG — 60 Harrah / 63 Horton

RT — 75 Williams / 78 Slater

TE — 80 Klein / 83 Nelson

WR — 81 Jessie / 86 Scales

RB — 30 McCutcheon / 45 Bertelsen / 32 Bryant / 33 Scribner

RB — 22 Cappelletti / 30 McCutcheon / 39 Phillips

SPECIALISTS—Punters: 9 Jackson; Kickers: 10 Dempsey; Holders: 16 Jaworski, 20 Preece, 11 Haden; Punt Returns: 32 Bryant, 45 Bertelsen, 33 Scribner, 86 Scales; Kick Returns: 32 Bryant, 27 Thomas, 86 Scales, 87 Geredine; Punt Center: 54 Reece; Kick Center: 61 Saul

RAMS' DEFENSE

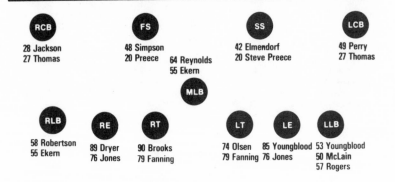

RCB — 28 Jackson / 27 Thomas

FS — 48 Simpson / 20 Preece

64 Reynolds / 55 Ekern

SS — 42 Elmendorf / 20 Steve Preece

LCB — 49 Perry / 27 Thomas

MLB

RLB — 58 Robertson / 55 Ekern

RE — 89 Dryer / 76 Jones

RT — 90 Brooks / 79 Fanning

LT — 74 Olsen / 79 Fanning

LE — 85 Youngblood / 76 Jones

LLB — 53 Youngblood / 50 McLain / 57 Rogers

INDEX

217

219

ROBERT BLAIR KAISER was a prize-winning correspondent for *Time* during the 1960's and still contributes to magazines in the United States and abroad. He is also the author of *Pope, Council and World* (Macmillan, 1963) and *"R.F.K. Must Die!"* (Dutton, 1970). *Melvin Belli: My Life on Trial* by Melvin Belli with Robert Blair Kaiser was published by William Morrow in 1976. He lives in Mammoth Lakes, California, with his wife, Ellen, and their six children.